# THE RIFT WALL

NORMAN CONTRERAS

9798393611699

When you tap the two locks with the heel of your hand because of the bush and try to find with your foot the floor lock to the door you know you're scared of the animals. But you did it in the dark of the morning over Ngorongoro, a lake like a small ocean that pushes the elephant and the lion into a small jungle against the wall of the mountain. How could you know she'd be standing outside your door, a blue kudu in the early light, and she spooked with the door and stood in the bush and all that was left of her were the horns like stalks of corn, immobile in the light and the shadow of the forest. You had a lot to learn about Africa, and you felt you had on your last night. You'd come to it with the fear everyone comes to it with, the strangeness of it and then the real fear of the animal and what it could do to you. The bush started to mean something when you saw after five hours what a lion in the tall grass can do.

You left Arusha with a vague plan to do it all in your head and you knew very quickly that so much was happening there was just no way to write it all down for later, the actual writing would never capture the Maasai children running from a half mile down the road for the boxed lunches and the watermelon and the bag of apples and one chocolate. "Asante sana" and he could only hold the heavy box and you saw right away a ghost of a line down his cheek and then he held the box and pulled the watermelon to his chest and stuck the wet part straight to him and you and Keto would laugh together driving the

LandCruiser that couldn't be shut off down the road back to Rhoti.

But the kudu. All the animals had been too easy, the elephant, the lion, even the leopard and the cheetah. The rhino was still a dream and you glassed the whole crater all morning and if there were 32 like they said, they were nowhere and even the silver buffalo from the dried mud, if they stood together the right way, seemed rhino in the right light.

It all started with a kind boy named Aziz you'd met in the Old Arusha Hotel. You didn't have the vaguest idea how to get to the animals and into the bush the way you wanted to, so you were going in the old way, that meant no plans, no guides, no nothing and just see what happens. It made sense to be scared, no one else was doing it this way, most people planned their lives around these journeys that were legacies handed down to them by thoughtful parents and proscriptions of class from a world you weren't born into. And how could they know you'd have the best ever with that hunt in the grass? Why even give it away so early how good you'd had it? Let it wait, kid, just let it wait. To hell with it, start with it, the rest will come.

Most of the LandCruisers of the safaris and the drivers in the Seronera of the Serengeti stuck close together and stayed on the common game roads to chit-chat and drive you crazy with the long talks and when you asked, nothing. It wasn't like fishing, captains shared, sure, the Spanish helped, but the real help was Aziz, the kind young man who got you Doudas and then it all began. There's not honest way to tell a story this close to having finished it without the honesty of the feeling it left you with, so if the story is still a little messed up, it's just the happiness not letting the calm of it get it down in a way that works for a story, it's just all too fresh, let's begin with Keto.

Keto liked to be early and he liked to be late. The morning of the lion he was early but it had to be a girl. He could drive crazy fast at the end of the day and be damned the baboons that stood in the way or he could drive as slow as he could without stalling in second, it had to be a mood thing with Keto, it just had to be. You'd talked mostly about women, like it always ends up being about when you're out on the ocean and why should it be any different in a LandCruiser solo with your driver? You were going to get as close as you could get to someone these seven days together, you were even going to almost die together and get burnt in the bush, what more could you ask of two men talking about women? It had to be that one was keeping him up at night, that had to be what was making him erratic.

He'd come early and when you walked out of the Serena lodge he was there. You just had to wait for the woven wicker box with lunch coming from the kitchen.

"Good morning, Keto, you sleep good?" He looked good, same shirt as two days ago, but alert and happy, he liked this as much as you. You'd learned this by now.

"I did," he said. "How are you?"

"I'm good, my friend. It's a good day. Did you hear the lion?"

"No," Keto said.

I'd heard it leaving a voice message for Lola on the balcony in the early light. This valley this early is as beautiful a land as there is, you can cry in land like this. It's a hard thing to explain putting something like this off for 51 years and then getting it. And being more beautiful than you could even dream about, almost... no, as good as the boat trip you took with your father when you were 9. Take my father out of the trip and this was even better than the 11 good years you had with your boat chasing fish off Macao. Imagine that, nothing but blue water and no land and the company of a good crew and to live the dream. Started on a dock with a Coke can and wrapped line and a spark plug to send it down and now this, the Serengeti. Good god, cry you fucker, you deserve it, 51 years to get it and now here. How to tell it, the two little warthogs in the grass, standing through the roof of the LandCruiser and not even Keto could see them driving, and all you saw was the white of their tusks. It was your first hour in the bush of the Serengeti and now you knew. Keto drove you up off the main road, to the east and some island playas of rock in the tall grass. When you get out here you understand why getting away from women for Keto made this thankless job worth it. He'd only been with tourists up till now and since you weren't one it was going to be difficult, but that's okay, you knew what to tell him and how to say it; how dangerous they could be, 'the real cats'.

But you got it because of the secret from the last book, it's too hard to say it, it's like talking about your father for the six years after it happened. You tried the first time at 14 with the girl that went with your cousin, and what was that worth? Where did that get you, yeah, it wasn't love, was it? No, not the first time, that's wicked to do it with your cousin, it's not on you, cousin, it was on her and she had a bone to pick somehow, and she'd found you, and you were just bad enough to not even tell her. Not tell her how you knew or how you found out or to even go to her. Just leave her, and watch at a safe distance. And now Keto, a good kid, a 25 year old kid just starting in this bush and you were leaving it… No, you'd left it and he was just starting. One girl, and a woman he didn't live with. Said he was Chagga, and his girl Maasai, that can't be good. And it took the whole drive to hear about the Maasai and how they were different. But it was only until you saw the women walking out of the bush with the wrapped cords of wood tamped to their heads. A lead Maasai just like a lead zebra, brave and not giving a shit. What man? Really, what man? No, the Maasai were like the cats, they waited for the women to do the work and then they came.

The secret, kid, it's big and it's the only way to make any sense of this. But it gave you this, the bush and now you were so crazy with it, you were going back to it after just 4 days in Arusha. Six good nights in it and back, you're a good man.

How can you tell them about the first drive, what the tall grass was like? That it was an ocean and as big a secret as you'd ever keep. The Sioux must have known it, and the Polynesians, and anyone in love with the big spaces, maybe a couple painters. How can you tell them about Miró out there? The line was right, the color, the space. He'd discovered it and given it back and if you were lucky you'd get it, this wasn't country it was a soul, and you knew it had to be free, the two warthog made you feel it. The lone hyena driving out with the bad mended front leg. You can't imagine *alone* until you see an animal out in this vast shit just looking, it's death really, and you'd had it inside long enough that it was coming out. You stopped giving a shit about the money and just had the people around you, your kids, that one good woman, your mother, not you. You were long past that. Now you were giving it.

The head guy at the hotel in Arusha wanted roofing, you were going to give it, "Why not?" as Keto would say. It was his best answer. Lumber and tin, why not? Past the safe shit and the fucked 'No's' and the circuitous meandering that's just a bad lie. Sure, you could just leave and not give it or just go and ask him how much he's saved and charge it at the supply store. You were like this now, and be damned where it took you, as long as you could do this and stay doing it, let it take you where it may.

Only pink 10,000 shilling bills for everyone, and for anything. Sure, they'd tell you if you looked it up that it's wrong, it's too much, fuck'em. *Gotti, Gotti,* keep it true, it's not where you got it and maybe he was doing it for different reasons but it's the honest way to be. And you were going down like this, you're last dive, kiddo. Now you're with Dad. And it just washed over you, just like with the grass on the right turn after the main road, you were doing it, after all these years. After just giving it and giving it, now you were taking it; just like getting out of the merchant marine... of anything. Anytime it feels new.

The fields went as far as you could see. The main road was crushed rock and if you looked on your phone map it went off to the right, east, and there was nothing, just the grass and after the pair of small white tusks you came to the wildebeest. Just standing, they must feel it out here, maybe a cat in the grass, maybe at those standing rocks, island playas you had them as, there must be something written somewhere proper about what they should be called, but you were past that. You weren't up against anyone, not when you're like this and it comes up so strong you'd feel ashamed if they saw you acting like this. Like a little kid, or when your uncle slapped you, or when your aunt got up in your face, you weren't big enough to take them on. Hell, it'd even happened standing-to in the merchant marine. They were looking for a charge, someone to lead the platoon. First they took to the kids the other one's liked, that was quick enough, and if not, they started asking, but you didn't want it.

And you didn't want it now. No, you were getting away from it, from all of it. Do you know what it takes to do this alone, this far, from everything? The grass said so, the animals were telling you so, maybe that kudu that came to your door in the dark, or the two elephant you drove with in Tarangire. Two big males, 40 minutes of shadowing them until the bold one came over and told you, 'Enough.' You will listen out here, trust it. No amount of wealth or success will have you out here. The only thing that will keep you is how present you are. How much time you've spent in your life with them. How closely you've watched them. How far you can take it; how far can you take it? Watch them. If you're lucky enough to not care, it's a beautiful song. They talk and they know, they really do. There's line out here. Old line, older than Chauvet, it's breath really. It's the meter of it. Don't get choppy with it, you'd learned that in the water at Puerto where your daughter was, inside, the water coming down with a chopping sound and you had to remember to breathe. And that girl in that book you wrote knew it. You had it. And it was here now. So were the 11 years on the water chasing fish off Macao and the Faro. Bless it all.

Fuck your old friends, just a place for your kids now, and you. Not measuring up anymore and it's cold outside.

The morning of the cat you'd left the voice message for Lola and heard the cat grunt. A big cat and it shocked you, the first time always does. Then you turned left coming down the hill from the lodge. It's hard imagining where a cat is in the sparse brush, small acacia, not the taller yellow ones and you came upon the clearing after circling behind. It was three hyena on an old kill, probably last night. The ribcage was larger than hartebeest, maybe topi, maybe something else. But not buffalo. It was the first time you told Keto to wait.

There was just enough water that you figured the cats might come back. Two jackal also and three buzzard. And it was early, the grass still wet and the flies bad, really really bad. Since you weren't changing your clothes out you were also starting to get bit on your hands and your ankles, but this was just part of it, so was the beard and the patch you plucked. Some strange shit you also did to your eyebrows thinking about the trip. You're alone, what do you expect?

"Do you see them?" Keto was asking about the hyena.

"Yes, they're big." You liked the way the jackals stayed close, they don't capture that in all the dumbass animal videos, they're always chasing drama, it's like bad books, always this compelling urge to have something happen, just cheap and bad. You were going to write new books. Absolutely new ones, and the rest be damned. It's the gift, the secret and the dive. Come with me.

Another reader yesterday, metrics says it's the girl and boy book, good god, can they finish it? It's hard when you think of the older readers and what they'd have to go through, but it's so violent now. Don't they see the kill? What's this age of, come on? You know it's death, we've got the Kyiv inside us, but think of the death out there in the bush, wanting what you have and how they'll pick you clean.

"Do you think they'll come back?" you ask Keto.

"Why not?" God, you have to love him, why not. Why not? You spent an hour on the kill and nothing came back and you left when the first hyena went back in the bush and drove out to the second road from the lodge and drove a saddleback with close cropped hills and good lion in the soft wet dust. They were walking the right way, but there was just impala in this part. The water and the sewage from the lodge was down here and some living quarters and when they came for water, they were always three. You'd even found where the guests could camp, but this grass and close short acacia was too dangerous and all that was left were the lights nailed to the trees in a close circle.

"Keto, would you camp here?" you ask him.

Keto just laughs, "It's a killbox," he says.

It took you awhile to get it. You heard it first trying to get out to piss in Tarangire, then again many times in Manyara. Just that Manyara was a true killbox, you knew that when you saw your first cats and the cat just laid there, you not 6 feet from it and all you could see in the short grass was a little brown from her head and the collar and the short round dark ears, a sick cat.

It's raining in Arusha today, a thick good rain. It's my first since Unguja. The eaves are thick with a long wall of water to the green garden. It all comes down in the end, it has to.

Now you know the killbox. This isn't just beautiful country for good smelling people to run around in LandCruisers and Keto knows this and is good enough to tell you. Get out and with the grass the way it is in the green season, you just might get hit, you might feel it and you might not, the fear may stop you from feeling it until you dragged off in the grass. Watch out for the green season. Whoever knew the grass? Makes Whit feel a little foolish, he didn't get all of the grass, did he?

The second road went on for two big beautiful brown and green valleys where the balloons would land and the blue trucks would chase them. Watching the young men fold the fabric in the tall grass was just hell and you felt bad for them. The owners were leaning the black bumpers of the trucks while they folded and pulled the balloon across the wet grass. You came to where the saddleback opened completely and now you could see more than ten mile down a gently sloping valley with a mobile camp called Ebon up on your right. The sun was good. The clouds even better, the sky very blue and a slick gutted, rained road that went down towards the main game trail. 6 LandCruisers at least, so it must be leopard or cat and then Keto saw her, she had just gotten up and Keto was driving fast trying to get where the other cars were.

"Wait," you tell him.

They were on the other side of a smaller game trail where a gulley ran when it rained, and he pulled over into a patch of shorter grass and we waited. The cat was huge. She began walking slowly with her mouth open and the LandCruisers started creeping behind her, all the people in them standing out of the lifted roof. And then they stopped, the cat stopped and then she walked again and we had her walking just past the front of us. Everyone stopped and the cat turned and looked and walked slowly past to a tree where she laid down. This all took minutes.

What do you say to cat the first time? 'Oh, my god,' is not enough, it is a different animal, not even elephant up close is the same, not even the big cat in

Ngorongoro breathing heavy in the sun and the breeze after the buffalo. Not even you.

This started the five hours you'd stay with her. Maybe you saw her first at 8:30 and by two she would hunt twice and no one would be there but you and Keto. The cars would come by and ask. Maybe Keto was feeling strange, but the cat would sleep for twenty minutes and then get up and look intently up the gently sloping hill. She had a lot of tree and when you saw them way up the hill, you knew. Zebra, she was waiting. Waiting was sleeping until the zebra came down. They had to come down. There were two smaller cat under a tree and you figured they were hers and the LandCruisers would stop and let their guests take pictures. She was about 100 yards up the hill under her tree and stayed there and you stayed with her and no one came except the one car and asked Keto. And Keto must have told them. They went right up to her and stopped and she never even got up, she must have known, and they drove around the backside of the tree and came back to the game road and left. And then it started.

The zebra had come down just enough and all the cars had left and she lowered herself in the grass and I can't forget what her black ears looked like in the tall grass, it's all there was to her. She veered off against the sun, the wind was right and she started as slow as she could. Sometimes she would sit for a minute and all you saw was a little of her shoulders and the ears if she lifted them to listen.

Sometimes you lost her for minutes and used the downed dead trunks to keep track of her in the grass. Glassing for her wasn't enough, you had to know where she was in the grass. Keto was quiet and it was worth the wait. Doudas had only given us one set of binoculars. She was still close enough in the beginning of her hunt to see her naked but after 8 minutes there was nothing but grass. It was a herd of 6 very nervous zebra. They were nervous because of the truck but they also seemed nervous with something about the trees and the way the land came down.

Zebra have a way of knocking their head when they're nervous, it's different from their normal chickenwalk way of knocking their head. They can stop and stare intently and if they're scared or nervous they won't move, they use the wildebeest for that. It's a dumber animal, Keto said, and they use them to cross in the Mara, just that there were no wildebeest now and the lead wasn't having it.

They were just standing in a clearing huddled and not moving and not feeding and knocking gently with their heads. The zebra were only beautiful when they walked in the bright early brown grass on the way to their herds and the line as they walked had the same gentle beauty of the giraffe as she walked past that you waited an hour for. Now, there was no beauty to them, they were scared and fidgeted shocked still in the grass. You knew they wanted something and they couldn't get the idea out of their head. The idea was going down and the cat knew it and now you knew that all the sleeping under the tree was waiting and her cubs just a stand of trees down the hill was a place they came to hunt. The zebra could go back up the hill or the wrong way across the grass where it was too thick and they wanted this one beautiful valley and they wouldn't quit.

They were so nervous they were starting to climb the hill again and the cat had shifted. She was so far that glassing her was more a thing of memory than it was of her. The only way to see her was if her back came up or she lifted her ears, and she hadn't done that for ten minutes. She'd been at least 15 minutes at it and the zebra had given up on coming down.

She'd gone way off to the right and you weren't even sure how she was going to come in on them. Keto was whispering the whole time and we were low using the bar on the roof to keep the wind from shivering her through the glass.

Glassing a cat properly was as hard as leading the school of tuna off the east of Desecheo. If anything taught you something about leading animals it was keeping those tuna up top and not going down. This meant a lot of distance and switchbacks. You have to flatten a mountain road to understand how to go back and forth at just the right distance to keep them moving, staying far enough away so that if the big fish come up, they stay just outside the school. Watching the cat was no different. You'd lose her for what seemed like the longest time and get scared of not seeing how'd she handle the end of the hunt. Watching each shoulder come up and her brown come up in the green grass was almost like losing your breath.

~~~~~~~~~

It really doesn't matter where you start. You can start with the topi gently going downhill while the morning fog burns off. You could start with Keto and how bad it got yesterday when he went full-kid on you and got the car stuck out of stubbornness. You could start with the tent next to yours and how the Kenyan was taking it all in. You could start with the locust walking slowly across the planks and the way the Frenchman's kids went crazy last night over a beetle. Or the way the bats chittered with the moths near your light as you waited for dusk. Or the southern Serengeti from yesterday and how you felt bad for taking Keto out so far when you got angry at him for the stupidity of getting the car stuck where there were lots of cars. Had it happened where you were, not even aerial reconnaissance would have found you before a week. And you were thinking of licking water off the rocks and eating the little bouncing birds in the short grass. Where do you really start? But you're here, my friend. Or do you blame the Japanese in the NatGeo hat, alone. He'd come from just as far as you, and walked off ungainly with the shuffling bed slippers, ignoring the tip box. Stay with the topi. Horns arched back, wounded birthmarks on their back haunches and down their legs, like something their mother forgot to lick off. And a strange bruised blue. Six of them, knocking their heads a little in the yellow grass, chasing circles in the shorter grass in the open plain where the sun should rise, but the fog won't let it.

And how you were trying to read it while you lived it. This is all there was and all there ever would be. He'd gotten it wrong with the hunting, it was right but you could see where he was losing the size of himself as he chose to write it. It was the same land and you loved reading about how he went into lake Manyara and shot the teal, and he might have been just a boy with Pops and POM, and how good Karl was. It was a long dive if he was 35 when it started, and you felt lucky for not having gone down yet. They'd tried as hard as they could with your kids, but you had Lola to thank for keeping your head up. It might have been the red manual she bought you with the keys that jammed. How could she know? How could she?

And you sat down that one morning in the house you built thinking that was the trick. Even built the portico the same, even thought about your father and the hell he must have had trying for it, even Old Vic, your grandad had it with the bullfights and living in Recoleta in Madrid. It messed up his youngest bad when he had to go on the meds for his back from the coconut in the Korean thing. How could you know?

Just yesterday you went back to where the two big lions were in the tree in the Gol. It was a good game road until it wasn't but it lifted a hill gently that let you stay with the two cheetahs you'd found driving the island rocks in the desolation. Keto didn't even see her in the squat bush that hung on the ground like a green Handel lampshade. She was peeking out of a hole in the canopy with her two week-old cubs crawling up her. It's a strange thing to be surprised by beauty like this, you could go on and on about how they gambol and how the French kids just out of earshot kick it up in you and how bad you miss your kids, and how you fell in love with your daughter the first morning you held her and could cry just thinking about her and how the boy, your little silverback, needs you to roll in the grass and learn about knives and wickedness so he can continue with the dirtiness of living and taking care of things, of his people, of his country, of their minds, if he's lucky enough to be stuck with it.

Because you were born with it, afflicted goddamn. And there's not a goddamn thing you've been able to do about it and it hurt even worse in your twenties trying to see if it would just settle down and let you alone. No luck, no goddamn luck, it was with you for life and the only medicine was the work you put into it now. And you were, you were giving it your all and still trying to live. The living had gotten easy, you'd been good at it since the promise. And the promise had given you not driving in the grass. Telling Keto, "No, don't go." Those damn beautiful cats you'd driven for were a half mile up the green hill on the great lone acacia, with a bent trunk that looked like a cat and you wanted to get to them oh so bad. And Keto had never taken the car off a game road and he wanted it just as bad and did. You were up through the roof, one foot on each seat and then you saw them. You thought they were mice, but they rolled a little funny. And then you knew they were some small birds that nested in the short grass plain and you'd have to drive over how many, kid? Just to get your lions up close and the beauty of the desolation of the southern Serengeti like a green ocean wasting away in every direction, and you didn't, for the small little birds. And you even told your mother about it and you left those cats and then something gave them back to you because not even an hour later you found more cats in the rocks and the next day when you got stuck sideways on the game road you got your cats in the trees and you gained something. You gained it because you weren't trying anymore, you were just giving it all you could and if no one else talked about their mothers or their kids this way then be damned–the ethics of it.

There were three softly rolling valleys, like yellow waves to the range in the distance. On these, sparse green acacias and bush, but not too much, just a sea of yellow grass as far as the fog and beyond that the sharp line of the range. You'd written about it 30 years ago, like penitents, their mouths up, you'd have to see them that way in profile. Be taught how to see that way through C Bresson and his gift and the hard work you'd put in gave it to you. It gave you all you had about seeing things, about the completeness of the vision and there were hand-counting few in this world that had achieved it and you were after it on this dive. Only one book about your country and the rest, well… what's out there. Go figure what plains these are and what fog is lifting. You're good enough, I know and I trust you.

The zebra are coming down. It's good to wait for these things. Waiting can teach you a lot. There's driving and pursuing and then there's this. With my eyesight the way it is, they're just white horses with soft black muzzles and a dark outline. A topi runs like hell in front of them, crosses the herd with foreshortened mime of trot and then stops and faces you. They've lined out now and I feel it, just like he felt it when he went to the south with it and said 'be damned everyone' and starved for it and left Verlaine for it and it was his best work and you know because you trust you are close. It feels right and is right and you're dying for it. And it's okay. They walk softer in this fog and knock less and look harder. They see the camp and are a good 500 yards off, an entire plain away. The Maasai are leaning the cut-in-half pirogue. The city Maasai with his gifted European boots with zippers, and the tall Maasai on his cellphone. A balloon is lifting through what's left of the fog and into the first patch of blue sky cut out with the fog. It's beautiful but strange.

On the ridgeline the acacias seem pressed from above, some outright fight others with a little more hope and bowled to the sky above. The most beautiful from here are not the leopard trees but the one arched up on either side and diffuse in its middle, it is me and it is us. I shouldn't say it but I have to sometimes, these things we choose to describe. There are too many rules and proclivities towards the accustomed and the righteous. I decided long ago I didn't want any of it, and this is my dive and I'll give the beauty as I see it.

Between the soft valleys, not a thick wood but more tree and more dark green to the softer yellow of the grass. The zebra and the topi gone, just the two Maasai and a porter in a mustard sweat and nice sneakers. The best part of the canoe is that, god, it must have come from far, you still want to fly over the Falls, maybe Olduvai and the real lake. You've no way of knowing if it'll feel anywhere close to what you think but then again, this is Africa.

When you try too hard it doesn't come, it's a big secret but worth sharing and not even close to your biggest one, but that one you can never give, it would make the world unsafe. Just give it as it lays, or is it lies? Come forth with it in all its glory. If you're caught up in sounding like it or loving it too hard it's bad and is off and we never forgive when it's off. All we want is you, to come out with it and give it, all of it until… Any more I give and I come to the other secret, that hill we almost made it to yesterday with no four-wheel drive and no one out there and the godforsaken danger of it, to be this far, this much in the south, that we were outside of the park, almost at the Naabi gate but with vast green plain with every animal but the rhino. And when we got to the highest rock island just past the strange rock that looked like a drunk Mexican with his hat askew and the eyes and the crumpled forehead and everything that made him so real you wanted a picture of the rock, you glassed for the 'waterbug' you hoped would be out there on the plain, skitting quickly, maybe just tapping his horn and chest deep in the grass.

Maybe he was better when he wasn't being cool, maybe it destroyed him, the fame and knowing what he had to give up to get it, his best work his first, and slow and studied and not an ounce of knowing what he'd get later but certain of its value, arrived.

I'll keep this as long as I remain undisturbed, I've no guarantee. A man with his family, a wife and two young daughters, one who shuffles her sandals as if they've got sand and smelling of soap so strongly I can

almost take drinking bottle water with the same smell
from the hands of someone who washed. All these city
folk coming back to this for this and not knowing and
when your spine tingled that first night in the tented
camp, here, with the grunt of a simba and the soft laugh
of the hyena you knew something, something older, and
something certain.

Because when you're trying too hard to give it
you can forget just what it is. It is the only certainty I
know, going on 51 and at 51 and his age and almost
certain my age. Three books in a nothing of months
since December and you are "working like you've never
had a job", don't think I don't owe you, I do. A
scratched blue sky now, the local family just about to
leave and you're back with Lola's kids at Barahona and
how good it felt on that mountain in the south of the DR
and how happy Lola was and how happy you were in the
room with her and how she tried her hardest to show you
and you loved her then and loved her always, for what
you had found with her and with no one else. Sometimes
you can hear it in children's voices, sometimes, now, in
the morning with what the rain on the tent does, that
sound, forlorn yet hopeful and what your mother's voice
does when you need it and what she felt like when you
held her and then smelled her and saw her eyes the first
time, a blue with no dark middle, blue all the way
through to your father and that trip that sunk you, oh
blessed.

There's no 'cool' to this, no other people, nothing for effect, just those little bouncing birds, so young and soft and disappearing under the LandCruiser and you couldn't stomach it, not for the cats, not for anything. It's what your father left you and what your mother raised in you and what's kept you at this, that little thing so easily crushed under something so big and mindless and struck with.

All these concessions to make it like something else, and you're beyond that, you are the hills now, have become them. Getting lost yesterday, almost, and using the tire tracks to come back into the park from the southernmost reach... and you can do that, just slightly, find your way with what you've left. The LandCruiser left just enough in the dried soil that if it went up the breach of the gutted road, there was darker soil to find your way back with. And it struck you, what you'd put Keto in and maybe now it's a good thing that you're staying in the bush in this tented camp and he'll go back to his city and Arusha and his daughter; you've always found a way to take it to the edge and he's a good young man and you've become dangerous and stayed that way since the promise and now this, giving it and hopeful, and Keto on the phone with a girl with a hope, after everything we've said about women, that he'll find it in them. But you want to tell him, no brakes, no four-wheel drive, no safari. It's the bastard in you, the real man, that doesn't care whether by lion, by thirst, or however, just let it.

It's growing in you again, just let it, that now you can make a life here in this tented camp and your work will be good and you'll have it all to yourself minus the day-trippers and you will walk these three fields and the three soft valleys. Already begun scouting hills to get to and imagined if you'll do it with the two Maasai, *Mr City* and *Lanky*. It will be all walked now.

The heat has come up, the fog all gone and the mountains and the ridgeline not yet clear 50 km away because of the low clouds. The brown backs of 5 Grant's just in the high grass run off hard by a cheetah maybe, you can never tell in the grass. Whit didn't know the grass truly, it's a mistake Ezra never picked up on and all the other ones were too traditional and too steeped in folklore to bother with, the grass is older than all things, it is all things, represents all things, word and writing and maybe breath, can you forgive that first movie with your father and feeling it when the grass waved, how best to understand breath without grass and fields and wind. There is so much.

You can only afford flights now and walking with two Maasai or maybe armed guard, you'll have to see. You need to be closer to the grass and understand it better and feel the wet of the morning on it, through your jeans, up to your boots and the wool socks you saved from Silver Creek. The bugs have come up with their screech, it's the deep south now, just like Yankeetown or a hotter road you stopped on for the first drive into México when you were going for your girl. You just couldn't do it any longer, the whole night starting with a blizzard in upstate Pennsylvania and then somewhere in Georgia on a backroad refueling, all those blessed cicadas and the hollering so loud it felt like craziness and you stopped and thought of things. Of just how crazed with love you were and were finally going into it, just like that day when you decided with the ocean who you were going to give it to and for what, and school had to go.

~~~~~~~~

It's strange being back in Arusha now, the rain is lovely, the balcony over the garden, the only place to work now. A lot better than the bush, you're too present in things with animals walking outside the zippered screen. There's no feeling like the topi or the troop of baboons doing their hop-run through the tall grass, waiting for the little ones that aren't sitting the small of their mother's backs or clinging with fists to their chests while momma slap-walks the earth with her hands. It can't be and isn't, this is a working spot, conventional and tabled and safe and just a beautiful green garden, wet and smelling like the mountains of home, an island mountain boy now.

It was easy dealing with Keto after the bad stretch, he understood it can only be one way and to keep us safe and the safari going in a car with three brakes and not even the linkage to the 4 wheel drive, it all comes down to the rains, we ended up driving out early yesterday for the Naabi gate. We'd come across lions late in the afternoon after the third hunt. We were coming home feeling good on our drive to the lodge and at a nice crossing for the game roads found them. Three cars on them and it was a couple mating and we watched them for a while and went home through the deep forest through a herd of elephants that stood us off and made us wait. The lead was pawing the ground without touching it and I thought it must be something mental, but when the three in the rear came towards the main herd up the road behind us, they shifted off into the bush and then met. The lead touched something in her and the pawing became a sort of anger the others must feel and we knew now was the time to continue. There was no way of even getting any closer than the 70 yards we had been to that elephant and Keto made a good decision keeping the car off, the way she would knock her head and just stand with the one foot up gently motioning was the strangest thing I'd seen in the 13 days in the parks.

But the morning, oh god, the morning. We'd gone back to the cats we knew that walked up on us. Keto was surprised as hell and he was still angry at me from what happened the day before and we had left late and got to the hill underneath the Ebon Camp that overlooked three valleys on a soft rise with two good roads that came through the zebra and one from where the balloons would land because of the big fields of soft grass and no brush and no trees. No one was there and the cats walked up on us with two cars following them.

"Oh, Norman, I believe you, you were right." It might have been the leftover anger drifting away and the surprise and the happiness of finding what we were looking for. I got so excited from his happiness I compared it to *matando recibiendo* in a corrida, when the bull charges himself onto the sword. I said there were two ways to do this, to chase them or wait for them. And because he was angry at me from the morning after I told him he had to go out and fix the car, at least add one more brake line to the front-right, the idea of going down a slippery muddy hill with one brake was just crazy and I'd had it and told him after getting stuck when we didn't have to, that the 4 wheel-drive needed it too. I meant: we needed, but I was really talking about the car and the roads.

She was as beautiful as the last time we'd seen her on the first day of the first trip almost two weeks ago. Her cubs were big and walked past the car and one climbed a small tree and jumped down and I heard the thud of his fat paws. The strange thing was the other cat, she was young but not as much as the two cubs. The mother had walked past first and walked right past the door I was standing behind and I got all of her back and she was as wide as a thick fish. Their backs were similar and strange, almost piebald with gentle discolorations like a black jaguar. It was two shades of brown and a dark stripe running along the top of her and her neck and her head was as thick as anything I'd ever seen. She reminded me of the first big cat I'd seen in Tuxtla Gutierrez 28 years ago, the square thick jaw and the pacing and the beauty of the solidity of her, it all came back and the soft sure walk of getting as close as she did to the car and the way her other daughter or sister followed far behind and afraid of the cars. There was no fear in her, the cubs just followed playful and gnawing at each other as they ran and tumbled into the rain puddles.

She was still a shy cat and young like a teenager and kept a good distance and looked at us and went off the path and walked through the tall grass and stopped once and then trotted on. When she got to her brothers they rushed her and they tumbled and they kept walking and then we followed them and they stopped in a deep drinking hole in the road where the wildebeest drank and got in and played like children in the water with their paws. We stayed with her until she walked into the bush and up a soft hill and then it was difficult tracking and we were lucky there was another family in another car who were also waiting for her to hunt and stayed with her until the onset of night.

Once when we couldn't find her for over an hour we drove up to them and they asked, "Have you seen her?"

"No," I said.

"Do you think she'll hunt?" The man was talking to me through the roof. I was sitting in my seat and this close we could still see each other and I felt a little shy about not getting up and being formal about it but I just didn't have a lot of trust in other tourists when it came to tracking cats. But their infectious drive to stay with them for the three hours we'd been on them loosened me up to them a bit and I began to love them as a family. I mean as the family I'd never had and always wished to have and to be able to share the things they were sharing. The wife then said, "I think they will." She meant the hunt. And I said, "Sure, it'll be zebra." They didn't know I'd been with this cat before and watched her hunt zebra twice in an hour and it had been the greatest pleasure seeing a cat do what it does and I'd become attached to her like no other animal and now I was seeking her out and had found her.

They had a son and a daughter with them and they weren't on their phones like the others when they drove past and this effort they'd put into watching the cats and staying for the hunt had made a bond between us and they cared. And that was a good thing out here, most of the cars just wanted their drivers to drive up on the cats and bother them. Even Keto had driven up on a cheetah we'd found in the Gol Kopje in the south of the park. The cubs couldn't have been more than a week old and still had that funny way of walking half drunk since their legs hadn't made it yet and they were clumsy and beautiful to see climbing over their mother when we first drove past.

It was an island on the southernmost game road and you needed dry roads and no rain to be safe this far away from the main road. We'd been lucky on the tenth Kopje and the island was stout and hilly sharp and it wasn't easy driving up. It was a little tucked behind one and the tree where she'd hid them was big but its canopy touched the ground in bright green on every side and on the back it was pushed up against a rock and there was one hollow you could see through that she walked across when she went up in the back against the rock the second time we passed.

I could tell by how she looked at us and the sound of the car when Keto drove up the second time she wanted nothing to do with us. I tried telling Keto.

"Maybe a little farther, and we can watch her." It was no use, he was too excited to see her this close. Later at the Naabi gate when I had to pay the transit fee with a big cat on top of the rock, the postings said 75 feet for the cheetahs or the noise would get to the females and the cubs and they could separate. It was almost as bad as the bouncing little birds when we tried driving up to the cats at the tree at the Gol Kopje.

I can't even begin to describe the Gol the first time we drove it. If I've ever felt being on an ocean on land this was it. Every little island and we got a little further south. And all there was, two lone buffalo and one giraffe and sign the elephants had torn bark from the trees and snapped some branches and little else. No cats, no big birds, just the rocks and the shortest scrub grass you can imagine. It was so far from the main road that when we left after we picked up the young bartender "from the lodge with the best rating," he said and I looked over and told Keto, "There." He agreed and all you could see was this hovering splotch of red brown that wouldn't sit still and were the last groupings or rocks; we'd gone as far as you could south, the last Kopje.

They were a beautiful family and had a good father for staying with the cats this long with us. Not only glassing but standing through the roof and staying there hour after hour and then you heard them when they found them.

"There! There!"

And then I stood up and looked. I couldn't say for those damned black flicking tails like Keto found because that came the day after, I was still looking for their heads popping up and their black curved ears. They were way up the hill and had lain down and only one would get up every so often and they never hunted that day, but the real find was that family. Of all the cars and all the pretend far-off stares and looking into phones and not even a head nod. Just strange, and the drivers always chatting it up and the one time we got a conversation going with this family the driver tore off in the middle of it. You can't blame him, but damn it felt rude and I really didn't like the guy right then.

It was the same shit that happened on the drive out with the bartender. When a car broke a leaf spring on the main road the whole crew was standing in the road and they asked if we could take the kid, Keto asked me and I said "Sure", I was looking forward to the company on the long drive to Arusha. He got pissy coming down from the crater when we stopped to have lunch at Ngorongoro. It's hard to capture how beautiful English can be when spoken the way a Swahili speaker can spin it so I won't try just yet, but I'd been trying to memorize just how Keto spoke and had even tried recording audio files on the phone to get the exact syntax and pacing but it even drove a young blonde from NYC crazy enough yesterday at lunch to spend 5 hours while I was writing, promising to bring his wife and child to New York. It's something truthful and pronounced, as in both definitions. It's like the words just bang out new the way they use them. I might even cheat and just use the audio file, it just seems a little wrong to do it that way though.

But anyway the bartender had none of it and he started off quiet in the middle seat behind and off to the side of me and piped up for the repair at the Naabi gate where we spent a good hour and I got dirty helping, I'd done leaf springs and still liked the idea of doing another on the road and finishing the job but the bushings were pressed in and it was going to turn into a 3 hour ordeal and we just didn't have the time. The bartender seemed pleasant enough at the Naabi gate and even knew about bushings and whether they were pressed in or just rubber stoppers you put in by hand or polyurethane. It's always good to talk shop with guys when they know their cars and I liked him then.

But when I told Keto to stop after the Olduvai crossing and asked about the museum you got the first funny look. It didn't mean anything then and you got out of the car and picked up the impala horn on the ground and got back in and they both got strange and said something about the ranger who just drove past.

"I can't do it?" I asked.

They didn't like to say no, or they can't, so that was the first look. The next one was after the pebble in the dust guard of the tire with no brake when we had to get out. Then the bartender got real chatty in Swahili and I'd had enough of it and told him in English, "I want to understand." I didn't really say it that way because I drew it out into a long joke where if he didn't, I'd let him out in the bush at the top of the crater. It's the shit the drivers would do that I could see bothered everyone in the car. I'd later ask Keto, "What did he say?"

Keto would just say, "We say nothing. It's just saying 'Hi'" but I knew it wasn't true from when he gave a car our first cat, the one with the two zebra hunts who we'd later track with the family I loved. I say *loved*, because I cried thinking about them and what they had and what I'd never been able to with my own kids. The Serengeti can do that, make you cry in the ocean of green. If you're coming to Africa for shit you're not even sure of like I was, you just might do it. Cry out there, try it, I even asked Keto about it and I don't think he got it. He'd never think I would and I asked him, "Like with the girls, when they get all emotional?"

"Sometimes, my friend, why not."

He didn't say 'why not' to this but it's something he would say if he knew and it's the perfect answer and the one you want to hear if he knows why you're asking. Maybe that's all you needed, let the badass out and just fucking rend. Tear that shit open and let it out. You'd come for the animals, the last book told you so and you even tried ending the book with the animals but it didn't come and you put it in the next book.

And it's the thing about books, you can lie a little to make it better, you can make Keto a little more Keto, and have him pop it when it needs popping, put that damn beautiful 'why not' exactly where it needs putting and it's why you're doing it and are going to die doing it and it's why you told that bartender you will do it and you did at Karatu when he didn't heed the warning. You told the kid in the nicest way, "English." And you'd tell the drivers too, and you'd scream it to the four winds. Keto tried waving the bartender off when he got chatty the second time, but there was no second time.

Because it's the funny thing about dying when you know it. When you can feel it coming on, I believe we know, all the highway girls at the truckstops know it, the kids with the needles in their arms, the boys at Puerto when it gets big and the sand blows out the back of the wave and my father when he took me on that trip I finally wrote about in the Spanish books. We know, we really do, and it's when we do our best work. We're not taking it with us, we leave it to our children, that they may do with it as they wish. It's our first folio, and our greatest gift if we're true and we're good.

So I let that kid off in Karatu and I told Keto, "I told him."

"I tried telling him with my hand."

"If he would have listened he'd still be here. It's what I asked him, 'All the way to Arusha?'"

"All the way to Arusha," he said.

"Okay," you said.

You'd made a big hole in the right side of your beard plucking but you still love plucking and it made you a little uglier and kept the girls away. Last night two that work the hotel tried the: 'Hello', as you walked past and nothing doing, just right on past and up to your room. Doudas came over for dinner and you even told him, "It's a secret, no one bothers you, they think you're destitute or crazy." You even said "destitute" when you shouldn't have, *homeless* just sounded stupid here in Africa and it's just an American word anyhow.

So you let him out and told him why, "Still a safari, my friend." It's hard explaining how they felt about us and I'd need more time, but there's nothing worse than a tourist, you should know you've lived for twenty years in a town built on them and it made everything bad. It made the kids bad, the baggers in Jumbo tried fucking with you when you had more sangre Dominicana than you could hope for, three kids and ten years fishing it and loving and even made Spanish another first language, you were going to show them in two languages. Maybe Borges could do it, maybe Fuentes. But you loved Unamuno and Arenas and Baroja for what he said about him. There's always a long list of books you want and you can count three you've read in places that made the places even better. Might have dreamt it, might have lived it in your sleep, Maupassant on Cayo Afuera, again on Prickly Pear when you rowed out to it and you found the African mask washed over and it sits with the mast step in your house and it's the only thing that matters now, and now reading him when you stopped in the mobile camp east of everything and you'd finally found it. What you needed to read so it meant something. You were taking this with you on the long dive, you just knew it. There're books and there's reading them this way. Sure you'd read it before, bought back in Ft Lauderdale when you bought the home and waited ten years to read after the stint fishing Macao and now you were again and it was finally meaning something. Manyara meant something now, the salt licks and the kudu meant something, the lorry meant something, even the old German journal and not liking the trackers when they got crazy with their shit. You had to live these things. When you really gave it and it was a dive reading it was the dive, going down together meaning something. There may only be a few readers left, maybe none, true ones I mean, that go into it and live it. You'd done it for México and found him lacking. There are those that give it true and then there's the mimes and the ventriloquists, the weirdos and the fakes. To do this you can't fake it and what it really is was being it, living it and coming forth with it. How many can say that?

It's the Kyiv in me that's got me all fucked up. It's the kids I haven't seen, and it's the ones I have seen, it's all the shit through the years, the giving it, the books, the reading, the wanting it badder than anything, it's the work of not having done it earlier and the guilt and that you came to it late, and it's the deepest of dives but the sweetest now that there's nothing left.

The cat on the hill, the cheetah looked at you that way, like 'why come and mess with it?' I've come all the way out here to this Kopje and there we were messing her up and I kind of knew and had to read it on some placard and it took the other cats, the ones that hunted the buffalo in the rain to know it.

It was our last full day and Keto had found them at 300 yards by the flicking black tufts at the ends of their tails under a bush and I still have a hard time believing it. The 'bush' they were under was a tree that one big cat had no problem sleeping in just one branch, that's how big the 'bush' was and it was big enough to sleep 8 cats under at that distance and still looked like a small bush. We stayed with them from 10 in the morning when we found them until the buffalo walked up on them around 2. Then they were all led out down the hill to the buffalo and we were so into the cats we never saw the rain when it came. And it came like a big thick heavy black cloud with just water. In a minute I couldn't see the heads of the 8 cats and when it really came down I couldn't see the buffalo either, that's a proper Serengeti rain out of nowhere. Just as beautiful as the one that was falling in the Ngorongoro crater when we had lunch with the bartender before I left him in Karatu.

~~~~~~~~

We'd been waiting in the car since the morning for the cats to show and I'd had a hard time staying awake glassing. When I did nod off, I'd stand up through the roof of the LandCruiser and prop my elbows on the roof rack and catch the little breeze and scan the tree where we knew they were. Going on three hours was as bad as it could get but I knew from fishing they had their time and it was going to happen near 2, like yesterday, so the waiting was easy.

It was like other things, a little like your work, every day with the hope that this one day it come and be there and stay and that you catch it, it takes a fisherman, that little boy while your father shot you with the AE1 when you swung the line off the Coke can and your father liked it that way. Don't ask him for sardines, hunt the dock-cockroaches or go down to the sand and wait, little antennas standing in the wet sand as the water flows down and a double heave of sand with two cupped hands and throw it like a voodoo priest and the sand whips across the dry part and there it always is, with bright orange *hueva* and they go in the plastic cup and they scuttle like dreams, eyeless soft sand-gray morphs from another Cenozoic.

Don't ask, kid. Just listen. And then the bird came down in the mud where the hyenas and the cats had left tracks near the stylus hoof marks of the zebra. A little bird with a worm from out of a hole in the mud. You were crazed with it and woke you right up, a bird in the mud. He pattered with the cute hops, no mud bird, a tree bird and went deep in the hole and came out and flew up to the tree you were using for cover from the zebra.

All the zebra had stood the top of the hill and their look had given you the cats. They'd stop knocking their heads and just stare as rigid as wooden horses and hold their ground and you felt good understanding the rhythms of the game, usually this took years without someone helping you, but you had Keto, but more than Keto you had fishing and the fishing and the waiting for the fish had given you everything, you were even hoping it'd give you the writing. Three books since December since you committed to English after a long ten year haul on Spanish and you had hope.

Then the secretary birds came through the tall grass at you, you'd only seen them from far off, at least a 100 yards, but this time when they came close the puff headed male had a beautiful walk, the most beautiful I'd seen on any animal. The longest legs ever, knees like ours, a long thigh and an even longer calf, the longest calf you'd ever seen, and the vibrating headdress, good god, a show every time he turned his head and the thin white blue feathers shook, he felt like something that would stop and shock big like a peacock but they just walked gently and purposefully through the grass to the road. They were very big birds, they felt at least 3 feet tall like the "bloody bastards", which is what I understood Keto had been saying until I looked it up and it had nothing to do with bastards and wasn't even a close homonym. I'd have to look it up to get the name right but I didn't really like the bird and wasn't going to bother, but the serval and the secretary bird were my favorites by far. Almost as much as the helefumps, which is what my mother had convinced me to start calling the elephants, hangabergers for–you guessed it, and basgettis. But the helefumps I fell in love with, it's as beautiful a word as any I'd ever heard from any child and it brought me back to my boy, my little silverback. All I had of him was the two videos on Youtube and some that I remembered and couldn't find in my Drive. It was the surety of the walk that told me he would be okay.

You can't really be sure you'll find anything like this anywhere, sometimes you find it in someone's walk or their smell, everyone's too self-deluding believing it's their qualities they've been shopping over and checking off the list when they sit over drinks or whatever. What it really is, is movement and smell and love. Not love love, but love as in cats, like when we drove up on them and where she goes he goes and they stay that way without eating for three days or 5 or however long she lasts like that. He'll stick with her until he's sure and then he knows. Why make it different, why even try? What makes us so different, I haven't judged them for what they did, I know they're mine and that means the world to me, and if I lose the teaching so be it, it's going in the books anyway and it will reach them, I know this. My little silverback.

You knew you were going to break writing right open, there was no doubt, the time was now and all you had to do was seize it, and you had. If it happened while you were alive, it'd be nice but it wouldn't change anything, what's been done is done. There's no taking it back, I'd been unleashed and no one could take me back. I'd even told my mother, "There's no way to control this anymore."

The little bird in the mud told you so–a little bird in the mud, you had to laugh, and you were, so hard you were crying all the time now and it gave you your work and with the earbuds in drowning out the business meeting on the verandah at Arusha anything was possible and you were writing it and you'd waited 27 years, this nutty dive and you were just halfway in the water, son. Father told me so on that trip and you loved him for it and mother had let the kindness you never knew you had in you out and all you had to do was break 'cool'. Sure they're our fears, they're all over. It's all fear anyway, go see the cats, if you feel your spine scrunch up with red electricity and the sound of the first far off growl in the mobile tent you have it. You've felt it and you're okay, there's still some animal in you, begin with the fear and work your way back.

As long as there's a little Kyiv in you and you're crazed enough to go into a war you believe in you're probably young enough and okay or old enough and still have it. If you don't, read, it will come, it should.

Sunsets help, Oman might help, maybe Goa, maybe Perth, or Cairns or the rising sun. It's an itinerary, sure, we're going east with it and when the girls in the lobby say, "Hi," just walk on by, go upstairs and sleep with the shades drawn and wake with it, it's in the red flowers, and the red electricity, a little in the water, and it's in your beard when it gets soft and sometimes a couple looks and kindness when it's genuine and your mother's voice, and here blue eyes the first time I looked into them in the falling light of morning in Oaxaca. Maybe the *chic-chac* as they daywage their rock in Manialtepec. You were changing it, all the boundary conditions of the genres melted now, freed through you of the constraints. And all you had to do was suffer and lose your mind and be willing to give it at any time. Meet this, it's unholy and uncontained and if it lives inside you, know this, the streets and the jails and sometimes, very rarely, the books, if read in the right places, seem truer than any drop of rain.

The kudu are in Ruaha and you're thinking of it. You need their blue in the morning, just like on Lake Manyara. A blue kudu for you, my friend, why not? Why not, Keto, my friend. You take these things with you, it's just like your mother's voice when she said "You can be anything," and you were. Or your father's beard, in the green glow of the compass off Mariel, a dream? Maybe a dream, a shock of black hair you wrapped in your fist when you rode his shoulders down

Cristo from the bar and the hoop in his ear from shrimping of Kingston and the soft ear, nibble that ear, son from the back seat of the red Thing on the way to Piñones.

They always want the story, every arc that got everyone where they were, but there really was only one arc and it was yours and it was the only one you could really know, all the others was faking. He'd been good enough to see it and had written most of his good books trying to break free of it and then it overtook him and destroyed him. Maybe, if you carried it further you'd be able to avoid the worst of it, or maybe you'd just be carried. And being carried is not such a bad thing, who doesn't want to go out on a wave?

For this blue kudu you were going to need the early morning light and closeness. It's not even light, it's what the mist does to the darkness, it's the water in the air, to say it's the light is to not understand the light. And you write fast, like you're not supposed to, and it feels good this way, unconcerned, you sprite, you. Flashing with it when it wakes, who's to know early mornings?

I'm thinking a lot about Cairns, it's hard to get big fish out of your blood. It's so strange when you think about something since you're a boy and you can't let it go, not even the boat and running it for 11 years in Cabeza and then in Puerto Real at the most beautiful marina in PR.

~~~~~~~~

Last night at the chicken place with Doudas you told him because he asked you that you'd do it. Just a little something to drum it up for the safaris. And why not? So you thought and you thought and two days on it and you got this:

*Don't go to Africa for the blue kudu over Ngorongoro in the early light outside your door. And don't go for black flicked tails of the yellow cats up the hill in the tall yellow grass that only Keto can see. Don't for the hefelumps as they flap their enormous ears and stare at you with their caramel eyes and you can hear them tear the bush with their trunks. Don't, but if you do Arusha. Arusha, Arusha.*
*Wanyama tours.*

It's all you could manage in the rough form, and with a little kinking and folding over and the sounds just right you'd get it. You knew you had it with the blue kudu but you'd known that when you started this. It's all origami anyhow, a little Tadeo revisiting you from El Batey. And Othello with beer caps and the chessboard good for checkers and now you're here with this, the rains of Arusha.

You can't describe rain in the bush on a tent. It's not the tent proper as they do what you did in your mother's house for the heat which is a roof over a roof, so the heat that percolates through can flush with the breezes. Same breezes Colón came over with and the same trades that took you with the old man from Radio Woso when the Murphys ran it or were they from channel 13?, no, it was the father of that kid with the MR2 you used to run around in with Randy.

There is nothing but trust, not now and not ever, just trust. It is the full-bodied expression of confidence and death. The secret is and always has been death, death and dying. How could you know, and why so late? At this, now, here. Come to you late and blessed and fresh with it just like the rain. And every slow drop on the canvas brings the topi and the hartebeest clearer into view and refracts further what was, what is left and what is not needed. The grass, the terrified grass, the terrifying grass and what it became when Whit wrote of it, how it changed from this, from the green season of Africa and what was needed were pilgrims and Quakers and homegrown soft innocence and now with this: the animals and what they feel and how they live with it, the way the zebras stay shocked still staring at it, their cats laying in the tall grass, and using the hills to stare down on them or the wildebeest to go first or the water buffalo to walk them down from it. You saw one buff with another behind go up to the 8 cats in the rain and push them off it. You were certain it was a hunt and you'd waited all morning for it and then the rain took it away.

You can learn from this, about going straight into it when faced. What, if not the lines of Chauvet could teach us about facing it, the purity of line? Stretched, it's your life, just line, the back of the cat. It took you this to get to the cats on the wall of the cave. *Homenaje* to the females on that wall, there's a reason there are only hands and just the bison and the cats and a woman. What school, what cyclics of ice this valley and this stone arch brought you this?

It's all reviews these days, it's what they depend on to sell it to us. That and the pictures. You still had that night in Abuito's house when you drove like hell to make it for New Year's when you were watching the animals and Oaxaca couldn't wait. You're lucky if you can find these pockets in this craziness. Lucky if you're crazy, lucky if you commit to the work, and blessed if you love it more than anything. But dangerous, if it ever leave you, everything else has.

Cayo Confites, don't forget, by way of Muscat, Perth, Cairns, maybe some south Pacific stops and Santiago. We need our churches, whether bodies or vials or beaches or bitches. No escape, think of the boundary conditions, a little roots on the earbuds, *'cause you never miss the water til the well runs dry...*

They're all pilgrimages anyhow, whether from your mother's teat or your father's rage, or your last love or the green grass of the Serengeti, or the boat you dreamed at the dock when he said, "Soon," when you asked. Why didn't you Dad? Why didn't you?

When you head out into it looking for it you just might find it, just don't complain if the wracked loss of what the storm left is not to your imagining.

I keep thinking about Cairns, and it could be driving things now, I almost wish I was at the tented camp again with just the rain. To want things, to drive, 'the procreant urge'—was it? Forth, forth... anyhow, it's a time past. Arusha is beautiful today, the president is here, there is no garden like an Arushan garden. I might go south with Keto for the kudu to Ruaha, and maybe three days to do the whole park of Manyara and finish reading the book I'm up against. I want to get all the cool out of it and the blasted dialogue and keep it whole, compleat, an angler with just his water and his rod. Pure, as pure as a boy on a dock with just his line and the hope. Anything you add is cool, I want the expectant wait, I want to be back in the Serengeti with the grass and the view through the zippered black gauze of the screen. I forgot the red electricity up my back for the published review for Doudas, and that I had it all before coming downstairs to start work. It's always better at night or in your bed dreaming it and going over it and plugging away as you freehand your thoughts into sound and the epic unspools and you're fresh with the salmon in the Yukon with her, the mother of your girl, and the young man with the long-poled net on the rocks after the chinook or steelhead and the bear when you drove up on them lumbered like furry brown shimmering rocks in the sun over the dimpled silver stream and everyone was there, every goddamn naturalist that ever was with the ridiculous lenses like apertured pickles and I hated it for the cameras but loved the bear and it took 24 year to get to Silver Creek and feel it again.

A kudu lives 8 years in the wild and 24 in captivity, and us? What of us? What is our captivity, is it as obvious as our lives and our comfort, or is it something more exotic, a deadening of the brain for not having gone proper to the mountains of San Jo for the 'shrooms and the wild living. For having rent and torn the very thing, what made you come undone, what's the levity to it? Do they just drink their way to it, how do they know, how do you? Is your path yet found?

When Momma got you that windsurf and you went out that day and got good and went out more, and more and be damned getting back, you remember trying with the boom and how dyslexic the whole thing felt, like touching the wrong side of your face in the mirror and you just went with it, out and out until the sun began burning the hell out of you and you were as thirsty as dried salt on the flats of Great Inagua and then you couldn't go anymore and tried laying the rig on the board and paddling and then you slept in the blasted furnace and drifted down to La Concha and were pushed in by the vagaries of current and fortune and someone swam out to you and took you in and you called Momma.

Taught yourself, young boy, to windsurf that day did you? And now this, north-central Tanzania for the same and you've always done it, on your own, even the writing, you know the guides, but the line you're casting is new and you'll die with it this time… it's a good feeling.

When you were in your honeyhole where the game roads met with the cats, a giraffe finally walked. And man did he walk, you were able to record with the phone the whole slow lumbering long-legged walk until he was right behind you, 13 second clips for Messenger so you'd get it good. It took weeks for the giraffe to not just stand under the trees and chew cud, the walk was glorious. It was your father's walk but it was a secret, so was his hair, and the bad skin and shoving his arm in the elevator doors to prove a point, and how he didn't do shit when Ari flipped you over and knocked your wind out from the full nelson.

How to say it, and still fold your skirts and stay proper?… dead, and alive with it, urged forth through it, a music of grass, dangerous grass for your cats, son. As wild a fire as ever was, no fetlocks of dug broken earth this centaur of you, standing it, your fire, while the whole thing rages, calm and benevolent, a Priam this river of us. Purple blue light and holy.

They tell you to forget your personal tragedy, to give it the way it is, and what way is it? We're moving this away from Kyiv and all the wars, we're going to have the courage to go after our boundary conditions, physics said it, give me a two body problem and the exact edges and velocity and I'll give you exact location. So if we fail it's because something has come undone, it is more complex than any two body problem, and another thing it's why they sound so flat when telling us the way it is. So, let's see... what way is it? What really fucking way is it, inside I mean, where our personal tragedy lies? I was watching *Alamar* last night on Mubi and I wish I remembered the personal tragedy of the creator of this fantastic idea: it was some thing of not finding the movie he wanted, so he built it. And I saw *Alamar* first in the Cineteca ages ago, but it must have been in 2012 because that's when the hiatus ended, the long one when I left Mex in 2001 and came back 11 later.

The boy and his father and his father. I'd have begun it on the pullback of the island, in every scene is the mother and the hard as shit difference of these two worlds coming together, the thing is, it's really three. The father of the boy never had his son, he made his life with the tourists which is a different form of catching, another predation, and the father of the man is pure, a real fisherman, disconsolate from love, from having lost and is *entregado* to the ocean. See, the man knows something, of loss and what the sea is and it's what I gave 7 or so years to that big book of the sea that was really an ode to my daughter and my son and all the others that feel it. If you do not fail in a book about the sea you have not written a book about the sea. So few, so few, and so beautiful, it's hard not seeing more having given it to the whale book or *The Islands...* book, they're good books, but because they fail, they become land books very quickly and it's unfortunate, the sea is about storms and other forms of consciousness and it sounds bad having to say it this way, the only way to write about it is with the water and a father and a son interacting on it. Wars, and hunting although nice don't mean what a life means as it's passed down to a son. I did the best I could with my daughter and had her go from Oaxaca to Gombe and then to her island world once everything had fallen.

"Father?"

"Yes, son."

"Tell me the one about the dog." They were up on the bridge pulling out from Great Inagua and the sleeper's plastics had a way of digging into his young back. He was burnt the color of baked chestnuts in Istanbul, his teeth white and yellow from not brushing, his father let him decide what he wanted to do and all he wanted to do was lay on the beach chair on the bridge while they sailed the old Texan's boat up. Dying's a bad thing when all you have is a boat to get home and a handful of pills for your heart and a kind man and his son to help you sail her north.

The night was bright because of the moon and the water held a mean silver streak that flashed and rippled and made it almost difficult to stare at, it would fade as soon as it rose.

"What do you think, kid?" The old Texan was looking at it.

"It looks good, I like it."

"Good to fish by, give it a try."

"Dad's going to tell me the one about the dog."

"Oh, yeah?"

"Aha, it's a good story, he gets shot and goes into the forest up in Alaska and he goes with the wolves and learns everything and he hunts and they get into all kinds of trouble, you'll like it."

"I'm sure I will, son."

"Come here, kiddo," his father said, and pulled him over next to him and pulled his fingers through the knotted hair his mother would love and Miss Rose would go crazy over making him spend the whole summer doing catchup after a month gone. "Cut that off, you look like a girl," she'd say. And all he could do was cry in the classroom and think about how good it had been. Cuba for the boatlift, Mallory square, Puerto Plata for the hailstorm, the big fish stripping clean the Senator you got in the drugstore and spooled with 200lb test, orange like the Fanta china soda you'd pop on the corner store under the eave with the rain if you were lucky and the horses waiting just by.

Just those shorts and the alligator shirt your mom loved you to wear. Light pink toenails from having been so burnt and your hand scarred from having held onto the rod from the big fish when he told you not to. You've got it bandaged and you sit on your father and take the helm.

"The night's different," he says.

"I know, Dad."

"What are you going to use?"

"I can't use the clouds."

"Look well."

There were a little bit of them from the moon

"Do you want me to use the compass?"

"It's better not to, it's always easier to use anything else, less strain."

"Yeah, my eyes."

"Look for it, son." He was pointing up, "Do you remember?"

"Oh, yes, the dipper points to… I see it. That's north."

"Yes it is. Now everything turns around it, you won't notice in the night, so you can't use another or you'll go off. It's just so you always know."

"Okay."

"See your degrees? Always check back on it so you know."

"Alright, Dad."

"Go get your father a coffee."

"Okay, black no sugar."

"No sugar," he said it again because when he wasn't popping his mouth full of the maraschino cherries he was eating a spoon of sugar, he just couldn't help it.

"He's a good kid," the Texan said.

"Hold up. Son, make it two."

"Okay," his son said up, going down the ladder to the bridge.

"Couldn't have wished a better one. Sometimes it's a dream if it's going good with his mother. When it's not, it's better he stays with her."

"You still do the late shift?" The Texan was talking about the bar where they met and he had agreed to help the Texan with the boat and getting it to Florida. No money and sick as shit and now they were on one engine. 42 Chris Craft, and it had proved itself in the hail in the bay of Puerto Plata. Not even the rat in the hold gnawing through the anchor line could mess them up. Nothing was messing up anything on this trip, that was clear, not rats, not hail, not one engine, not nothing.

He was tapping the cigar when his son came up. "You take her," he said. "Let your father talk a while." He got out of the seat and his father stood and he sat at the helm.

"What do you want to do about Cuba?"

"I like the idea," the Texan said.

"I do too."

"It's not bad money."

"No, it's good money. Damn good money."

"Just the radio."

"Yeah, just the radio." The shrimpers out of Key West were saying what they were doing to some of the captains.

"It ain't pretty," his father said.

"No."

"Well?"

"You tell me," the Texan said.

"The boy. My boy."

'The boy will be okay."

This boy would always be okay. He's one of those boys, 9, that was always okay. Whether he flew off superman from the wall and landed blown out on his chest, as knocked out as if punched. Or flipping two cars, or the guns, or the machetes or all the shit that was waiting down the road.

The old man was waiting and his father knew it. It's one those things you think about and he thought about all the shit he'd been through and what had gotten him that way.

~~~~~~~~~~

The more you watch something the more you know it, it's like that with the cats and it's like that with

Pereda, and Huezo and now *Alamar*. The more it gets reduced to its essence, the clearer it gets, water, rivers, silt, wind, these things in stories can be as permanent as the author or they are the story.

Leave the mother out and just let this boy work out with his father what needs becoming. She will take him and show him the ways of the city and pull him back from the poor life. Don't they all wish it upon their sons, the success, the good life? It's a poor life, that of the fisherman. But it's not a fisherman's tale that way it's told, take Europe out, like Fuentes did and Paz and let it stand. Let these men be what they will become and there you have your story.

When the father tells the son he will be with him always, whether in Rome or anywhere, you have all the background you need, and the snickering of the fisherman on Chinchorro for "*Papi.*" Something has been torn, because of the outsiders. If you have ever spent good time amongst fishermen then you know. The hardest men that ever were, the original Oedipus. Not a carpenter but a fisherman. Let it gel, all of it. There's enough to think about with all the schlock committed to celluloid about water to just leave it as it stands. It's why it's so hard to do things about the water. It's the same with translation. Every time I read the books and see what they've done to them so my daughter can begin to make her inroads I'm undone with it, the horror. They cannot for the life of them understand what they're bringing in. You must work from the language you know best, there's no other way. Borges understood it, when in the interview with Buckley he gave up on Macbeth. He just couldn't do it. I'm not saying you shouldn't try but you must try, with all the heart of you, they deserve it. The greats deserve it and more.

And so I don't buy the books for her, it hurts because you know it's the only way to make sense of the others, whether it's culture or people or other minds. It's why we do it.

~~~~~~~~~

And you felt guilty as hell for the 'procreant urge', for having arrived, and had the gumption to know it, who?, what other? You know, and have known, born this way, sure of its arrival, not even needing an Emerson for the doorstop. Known from birth, lover of book covers and smell of page, and now... of grass, true dangerous yellow and green grass, and Afar and Olduvai grass of hominid first steps, and still with the wave after the Scotch & Sirloin to walk up the steps to that arthouse where Kurosawa's grass did wave, and still alive with it and genuflecting no soul but your own.

Yesterday and into last night with Doudas at Africafe. It's a funny thing when you get exactly what you want the whole time, from birth to this, through death and children taken and now you know. It's the luck of the draw, the two straws you've been drawing your whole life and now again, you draw the longest and like telling Doudas, "I don't know how I always get what I want."

You were telling him despite the lack of 4WD and one lost brake on the front right tire and Keto being all of 24 and acting it you still managed the three hunts in the green season.

"Do you think anyone else got that?" You're looking at Doudas and you're not sure if he gets it or he even cares, he seems like he does but it's always difficult with a businessman and one as good as Doudas, but you enjoy his company, Tabore and the far northwest of Tanzania have made him a good man, stealthy but good and wonderful company. It's not often you can spend 6 good hours with someone and laugh and hold court and tell story and listen. If he were Chagga it might not be so easy. When he told you about how he survived Covid in the bush on his 20 acres cutting maize and by flashlight spooking the pigs that came to take it, you knew, a real dude, anything to keep his family good, and you loved that about him and when it clicks you know you're good.

~~~~~~~

He wanted it as bad as he'd ever wanted anything for his son. From the very first days of telling him you're born dying. And you were really, from the North Star you were using for the dead reckoning westward from Great Inagua.

His father was looking back at the wash from the one engine after they'd lost the other from bad fuel and the storm in the DR.

"We're going to need something to handle the men."

"We may not need men, they say there's women. We could take women and children." The radio was going off with what they'd done to a couple shrimpers, old-timers a little too trusting but after the easy dough. "The boy will be okay." He tried again with his boy but it was something else.

"I know my boy will be okay, that I'm sure of."

"I'll be okay, Dad."

"I know you will, son. I told you that a long time ago."

~~~~~~~~

The bush when you're in it is almost like water when you're diving. Just the way you were the summer out of the merchant marine when you'd go turtle to the first reef, then the second and finally the last one before the water got too damn deep to gently push your chest across the sand on the bottom and come up for air. It must have been the same for him when on his second safari he started doing the night walks and heard the lion and saw the wildebeest and kept good with the nightbirds. It can't be that different when you're in it. You have all this all the time, the thickness of it, it's almost like Istanbul when you walked the bad part of the city and got lost, how you could feel it until you saw, huffing a corner after the steep climb and the guy on his scooter saw you and you locked and he wouldn't stop staring and then you knew, it's the same shit as back home, what a stare can mean if held too long and you weren't giving up yours so he went into the business he was caretaking and that was that.

~~~~~~~~~

"You know, son, there may never be another like this."

"I want to go, Dad. I really do."

"And I just might take you, it all depends."

"Jesus, what does it depend on?"

"Don't say Jesus, I already told you."

"I know, I'm sorry."

"The Lord's name, never in vain."

This was old Catholic shit he'd pull when I was a kid and it's one of the few things I can remember other than Father Bernard who he used to drink with and according to my mother was as good an Irish priest as you could hope for on an island, an honest man who could hold his liquor. Then there was Tufiño, the painter, and Rafa Pons who I only remember from his mustache in the back of the red German Thing my father drove around in without floorboards from our beach days and not toweling off after getting out of the water. The same one I stacked pillows and books on the seat for the skidding figure eights out at Piñones. It's all I remember about the damn car other than losing it just like the boat to San Juan Bay Marine when I lapsed on the monthlies after Mom forgot to pay it. What do you expect out of a 10 year old boy and a bereft mother? God, it was a beautiful boat, a little handmade whaler out of Bequia signed on the mast step by Lincoln Oliver. I rubbed that damn wood with teak oil for years after losing the boat to the sailors that bought her for a song as a dinghy. I can still see it leaving, tied like a bucking donkey behind the big old sailboat and reluctantly leaving me. I'd managed to keep the sail and the rigging in the storeroom of the Port-O-Call where I'd gone years later to meet the cousin of an attorney friend of mine from México. It started as quarters for the pinball to this, a sly get-together for nothing more than felony wickedness on our part, but what do you do when you feel like being bad and it's something you share, even the wicked share once in a while. And she was a good woman who had some preternatural gift for reading me and said it out of the blue once, as if she understood my pain and somehow did. Had known it, I believe, from the second she met me in Fubar when it was still on Ashford and not moved to that god-forsaken shithole out on 65th.

There were good people who went to the bars in PR when you were young, Fernando, who shot himself, and was a good friend of your fathers. Davy Jones, the old partner and a whole hell of a lot of dead others from a different PR when the road out past Canovanas was sand and the ancón across the Río Grande de Loíza was worth waiting for. Long before all the cheap-ass cars came when no one, and I mean no one, had Mercedes. PR was a poor island where if you were lucky they'd pull out a Philips on you and ask you for your bike or finagle a skateboard out of you as a trade and then offer to go see what happened and you'd lose your bike and the skateboard and learn something about the kids that didn't sniff glue. About being sly and you still have the pregnant girl in your head that used to walk Teniente Lavergne pinching her nose the same way Jessie used to when she slept. There's all this shit stuck in your brain from growing up on the best island that ever was. Fuck, and if Joyce could do it for his Dublin, why not you? No Joyce they say, fuck 'em.

The glue got 'em. And if it wasn't the glue it was the dope, they snorted the whole decade in or they fell out in front of Pinkys with the fentanyl so deep in their gray matter there was no room for Agee or Evans or the poor of the Dust Bowl to work its wonders on you between class CD Wright and walking down Thayer to get the Paris Review and vomit up the Caesar salad in the bathroom because the hepatitis from Puerto got you down with the chalky yellow eyes and you couldn't even go up a flight of stairs without being as winded as a preggo and you still remember her good thighs before Mar was borne and you can't forget Byron on Ashford wanting the good girls from St. Johns and maybe even crying over them and what's left are books after all this, little petering wisps of thought after the death is done and the crazed have gotten lost and those that were destined to die did and it's just you and Arusha, waiting for the rain and maybe a flight through Doha to get back to your mother and her 78 good years to make sure you gave back what you took.

~~~~~~~

"Goddamn did you take, son."

"The lord's name, father." You were fucking with him in your head, you wanted him talking this way for some strange reason in the story and it made a strange sense off the coast of Cuba, Cuba always needed God and sacrilege. It had him, and he was good for Cuba, as good as the liberators, but not as good as Arenas. You had that, at least. A whole afternoon with *Antes que anochezca*, you still have the thick cotton throws on your clean back after the shower and how good the room felt with the ceiling fan wheezing its slow *whoop whoop* while you gave the book all you could. He took you to the parks and you finally felt summer the way you had summer in PR. No one had done summer better in the islands than Arenas. No one had done a small cove and shorecasting better than da Jandra. And what's crazy is he didn't know it. The only thing you did know is what you were doing was a breaking. You were tearing the walls down for good. Built up for good, or so they thought, and now all was one. Again.

You had one other thing that kept you in that room all afternoon, and it was the kid you all jumped in the Iguana. You paid for this afternoon with blood. The blood of coming for you had it been what you thought. But, give an afternoon what it deserves, a good book, and you have the world.

"The world, son. The whole world."

"I don't want the whole world, I just want to go with you."

"And you will, in time."

The dock was cruddy from the oil of the sardines, and the leakage from the pine. It was a bad smell that you loved, a dock smell. In the DR it was burnt diesel which they used to cure the pine from Pico Duarte. You still had what Puerto Plata had left you, and you'd have to go to the Spanish book to get out what only Borges knew from Macbeth you couldn't, so you didn't bother but you still loved the hopefulness of trying and you still loved the story the same way you loved the contact sheet he took of you on the dock, the one with your hand out and the gentle parabolics of line whizzing out past the hands, it's almost the bubble in Alamar or the bottle floating away with the note. The same one you did, with a wry riddle, a small jest of, "How do you make a Y with one finger?" God it was beautiful, and you may have drawn it... "You did, son, you did."

"We're going, boy."

In the Spanish story you have some gay shit about getting hunting weapons in el Club de Cacería in Havana and it always felt wrong and you'd fix that this time. How much could you with what was left? There was Kyiv and what it had done to you, there was your dead father and the kids you hadn't seen. If he was right, there was Pound and there was Joyce. If you were right it was time to bring it down, all of it. You'd done the American book; it was good, better now, thinking about it, than you could have hoped. It had the best love scene you'd read and you'd read good ones, not great ones, but very damn good ones. Not the patrician shit from the midwest where he'd got it all wrong, not the Pauline Reage *O* stuff that was pandering but the true dynamics of power that shift and ebb and the flow state of a true interaction, the sex was the power. You'd gotten that and the damn beautiful shifting in us where it can change; you'd still liked *The... Eden* book. Something had been gained there, it was a new shift, so much had to do with possession and power and dominance and the shedding of it, you'd been in enough of them to know.

"Pa, when will we go?"

"We're going in at night."

"Late?" you asked.

"It needs to be late, hold on, son. What are they saying?" He was looking at the Texan.

"Something about the harbor. I can't make it out."

We didn't have charts of Cuba, only the lesser Antilles and the Bahamas. All I remember him saying was something about Confites which was as damn east of Mariel as you could be and still see some glow from the cities.

"It's all a thousand a head," the Texan said. He was squelching the radio proper and even I could make out '*a thousand*'.

"It's worth it," my father said. "We can do thirty, women and children." It was the same way he talked when he said about his arm in the elevator door with the hard rubber stop that almost crushed it and the first time I saw him wince. It's a lot of pain on an arm. And he still gave it and was going to die giving it and it's what I kept telling Keto about children. His Chagga ways sees him with his daughter, 8 just like mine and the mother nowhere. In their culture they take full possession of the child to make sure she grows up loving her father. The only thing is, not him, his sister or an auntie or the mother. That way it's allowed, "a grown man with a young daughter cannot be in the same house living," it's kind of the way he said it, but I just don't have the inflection right–his beautiful Swahili grammar.

My father had his eyes screwed on the compass and a westward bearing, in the story I have them come upon the flotilla floating with yogurt cups with candles but that's not really how shit happened. They talked with some young guys.

"Dime, Viejo, ¿cuántos quieres?"

"Treinta," my father said.

"¿Seguro?"

"Muévete." My father wasn't up for his shit and told him to get a move on. He'd come out on a rowboat, and the kid rowed bad and had a way of slapping the water that made us flinch a little. It's always better when an old man rows and does it well. Where he'd gone wrong about his Cuban stuff is the rarefied world of pigeon shooting, trap and all the other country club meanderings that had him believe he understood something about local folklore. Had he gone out on a skiff he'd have understood no man waxes heroic on the ocean, no true man that's lived a life on the sea. They're all crusty old seamen with bosomed posters of girls draped over the hoods of cars and they don't fit in enough to have a home life with all the trimmings like kids and wives waiting; the true misfits and malcontents. And if I were going to write them right, which I promised from having lived with them day in and day out, I promised the real McCoy, real fisherman the way real fisherman talked, and it wasn't pretty and hadn't been.

My father had known a couple of traitors to his class–I might have gotten this from Mubi watching the Vidal/Buckley debate–who went to fishing from law and good newspaper work from the Star when it had won some Pulitzers on the island when we still had a good paper. The attorney had gone into it for the love of it and to get away from what he saw as a bad life dicking around amongst the shitheads; he wanted it pure and he got it. I first met him at the fishing village down through la Puerta, the old city wall's gate I'd walk through coming down Caleta de San Juan where the cat piss stench drove you crazy but it was still the most beautiful street in the old city and back in those years the only street that meant anything because of the big tree that tore up the blue cobblestones and made it hard to walk down. This attorney guy promised himself he was going to make a life of it and did and my dad took me to meet him after I asked for a dollar for sardines. I'd always walk all the way down the seawall and loved walking into the gate of the village where they each had their own shed with their hanging everything: nets, lines, the propped up motor and always a little cot amongst the floats and wickwacks and I loved it. Just walking past the numbered sheds, all the blue doors to the long cleaning station of hand burnished cement with the one long, very strong galvanized tube with the water spigots they all cleaned the catch on.

I'd made a joke out on the dock with my friend who came over on weekends about the governor's turds that washed out of the sewage pipe on which the dock had been built which had caromed off on a northerly groundswell. The fishermen didn't give a shit and launched their boats or kept them tied to off of moorings and always rowed perfectly out to them, nothing like the young guy in the story. If you want to see poetry, watch an old man row who's done it all his life. Forwards, backwards, standing, sitting, all of it–it's the preamble before the true drama begins and it has to be tinged with all that expectation and Thanatos, that what he's about to give, he's given it his wives and no good, his kids… and no good, all that shit in the city and nothing. All he's got is her and he's going out to her. You see, there's no way of capturing it, it's loss, it's not Shakespearean tragedy, it's not comic, it's nothing ever properly captured for having not been lived.

And you were giving it, in the story, in the book you had, in the bush, standing through the roof watching all the green grass on that first drive through the Serengeti when all you saw were the two warthog at the first Kopje. I'd never felt such beautiful desolation on land and then I forgot all about it being land and began with the ocean feeling and just changed the colors and let the wind do the Kurosawa thing to the grass and lived that too and said, "Now, I've got it again," after all those years and having to sell the boat for my little girl and the damn penance of not having a rig to take her out on when I finally got her or my boy in the Cono Sur.

"Muévete, coño," my father said as the boy paddled off. It helped, he figured, I know that now, that he meant business and wasn't about to take any shit. It has the emphasis of: "Today, motherfucker!" And when he did finally come back there was a bigger rowboat and they only walked slowly with one hand out steady on the gunwale to step on the boat. My father was helping them up one by one and he didn't ask about the money and cared more about their footing and that they didn't stab a shin kicking a last leg over before they came onboard. The Texan was up top on the flybridge patiently waiting, there was none of the drama or fear of being hijacked or having our throats slit like in the book, just my father's old patrician care that the women got safely onboard. And they did and I never saw how much money or if any was paid and we left.

They were all a little like the dockboys I had met in Puerto Plata, except they were very little boys and girls and very scared and very poor and they stayed very quiet and went down below and sat in the cabin on the furniture or the carpeted floor. There was no trouble of any kind and we had a quiet and good crossing to the Keys and I don't even remember that much about coming in. I do off the docks at Mallory and pedaling around Key West and the backroads and what the haze was like in the living room at midday with all the hippies getting stoned and how I'd made a new home here on the island and never wanted to leave.

There was a running joke about my mother and how we had to call her and kept putting it off and promising we would. It all started at the seawall on Great Inagua and the dusty coral path. It continued through San Sal and Nassau and maybe Little island and all the others we stopped at. But the joke was on us, she'd sent the Coast Guard after us after the promise of 10 days had worn thin after 30 of having been gone. One boatlift and one badass storm later and we were still whole and I'd changed for the good. I'd always known it was going to be a project to get my ass back in school and give a shit after a trip like this and it never really was the same. I'd been smart enough to use it though when I got the blackass at 15, I liked to call it "my midlife crisis" to my friends and made a promise to myself that I came first, long before the ungodly weight of the bookbag with all the schoolwork that I got progressively more behind in until I stopped giving a shit and just focused on the water.

I started with that damn windsurf my mother had given me and went out with Randy in the afternoons and sailed all around behind the small cay in back of the building. It was a mean ocean when you got out that far and the open ocean swells were hard as shit to jibe on, you always had a way of losing your footing on those old ten foot boards, the first windsurfs that weighed 40 lbs and were hard as shit to carry under one arm and hurt the top of your head if you balanced them up there. These were big open ocean hefty dark blue swells that had you thinking about big fish if you fell and bouncing right back up on the board.

Even all the way to Ponce when you took four 1sts and it felt damn good not because of the 1sts but because it was open ocean sailing and you didn't fuck up on the swells jibing or tacking the markers and everyone else was eating shit because of the long period swells, you'd nailed it down and it was worth it, all those afternoons after school out there getting it right. It was a beginning, of just going out and doing it and shedding the fear and making sure you got something down that you needed, it was the same thing you'd need in Jamiltepec and the caves of Cayey and Puerto when it got big and just walking the streets of Zipol with your crew and staying safe in the streets of Oaxaca and now this, the Serengeti and in one day Manyara done proper.

What he'd written about it when he went swimming and shot the teal and loved it the way he did was needed now. You hadn't gotten it the last time you went, it was the first damn park and you stopped for the baboons and Keto was being a prick and just trying to go full tourist on you and now at least there was an understanding with Doudas that you'd do it proper, so you had three good full days in Manyara and you could even do a night game drive but that depended on the moon and the cloud cover.

You just found out he stayed here, as well as Roosevelt, how to know you've become infected with it and it's in the air and in the garden. It always has to be the garden, of all the hotels you've been in, and been living in these 30 odd years, this is the garden that sets the standard, it might have been that, it could have been the way the birds used to fly in to the Caribe Hilton and walk on the longest mahogany bar anywhere and the open roof with ninety feet of good tropical breeze flying in. We are these gardens, Arusha hotel, here's to you and not knowing how stuck we were with it.

It's a strange thing we do when we build our gardens, the gardens are our books and our dialogues, the hardest part, the bloody architecture, what we leave after all these years is nothing compared to the gardens, each succeeding generation of talent redoes the garden, the big trunks standing and the smaller ones. Oh, Lola's garden, didn't you see it there, you devil? Lost that love, did you and here you are with some strange dementia of picking a bald spot in that beautiful beard of yours while you give this garden and this veranda all you've got, last laptop taking it like a champ, the two previous others with Aziz now, the cracked one and the one you wiped to give to him.

Just this, the sun in the garden as it comes down and the light you've been trying for all these years. No one's gotten the light, not ever, the light and the water are the mysteries. Have been the whole time, *shake-a-spear* almost got it, but damn that collective of talent and professional actors, what they were after was the exchange, like gasses in some Archimedean flask, not the light nor the water, was it *The Tempest* and Caliban that his son tried so hard to discuss to get at the problems East Africa was having and how it could get your head lopped off if you weren't careful? It feels the same way now, the same quiet desperation because of the wages and the stories you have to hear about roofs that need paying and an Auntie who raised her with the asthma and the cancer in the pointed throat.

She's a nice freckled sweet albino that you love talking to. When you asked her, she said Helen is the name of her auntie. What a beautiful name, the most beautiful and the closest to wind ever. And war and the impermanence of it and what we're willing to risk and surrender to go forth with it when needed.

It's strange when you start falling in love with a girl, it happened with Ezra in Istanbul and now her, it's happened too many times to remember, you have your solid women, the ones of the long loves and then this proximity, of the stories shared and the nut finally cracking, it all takes time, only this, the living in it, day to day, in these hotels does it happen. It happened last in

Sanborns when she got pissed at you when you finally asked her out because she wanted you to. And when there was that certain Latin bullshit they start when they don't want to give it, the little game they play to get you hooked you didn't give her another shot. You still remember describing walking the night to Bellas Artes and then the no reply, ghosting is it?, fuck 'em. You've got one shot to keep it honest, after that, all bets are off, my work means too much to me, the world does, the things in it and the goddamn brevity of it all. I wish I were healthier to give myself the lying guarantee that it'll all be here tomorrow. I don't even know anymore if it will, that's the sleep I have now, take it my sleep, you gave it all those years and "then you took it away", god, Bukowski was beautiful when he said it, the first and only flesh poet, better at saying it than writing it, and no courage big enough to lay it on them when deserved, him and Miller. You're a halfwit if you even try in the halls of academia. And you left, left it all with that jeep in the forest of Lynwood at your buddy's house and how you drove that cold-ass blizzard in Pennsylvania.

And what the lady said the morning after, after driving the whole night straight through, blue ears, a hand that couldn't pour that damn mug of coffee and two legs that couldn't stop rickety-racketing the clutch with their shivering. Couldn't even hold it on the gas pedal, a *vroom vroom* unsteady acceleration and you said, "Fuck it!"

Just stopped and the lady said, gently at first, "Look at you, is that your car?"

"Yeah," you said.

"Are you going far?"

You didn't want to say Mexico, it sounded too crazy. "I got a ways," you lied but didn't. Mexico ain't no ways, it's the end of the road.

"Where's your top?"

You had driven it out like that, with just the bikini top and the real top was folded in the back with the half doors propped behind the back bucket seat.

"It ripped," you said.

"Oh, poor you, what don't you stop, there's a place right there," and she pointed. A little blue motel with a couple rooms. It was some mountain town. You knew you had to and did. Nothing happened with the lady, it was just motherly concern, it's what 24 and a young clean face does to women. It might have even happened to Stein and Beach in Paris, hell, I don't know, once you start giving it, there's no way to turn it off.

It's ironic isn't it, that in the story you're off Confites with your father, sailing past, sure, but you've been there, been a whole hell a lot of places you wish you've been and sitting down and writing it you realize, damn, you've been there all along. It's that strange circularity of the story, the true story, where we leave to come back from whence it all began, but you're more generous than all the others, a little more noble and giving. Just gave 30 thousand shillings to the girl to go see her auntie as you write this. It's just you and all your glory and the balancing of it, the damn bush you're trying to die in, the people you're coming across as you fjord this damn beautiful country with all its heartbreak and what you have to do to keep the sly proffering down to a simmer, if not they'll come with the whole shebang of story and leave you bereft of everything but a phone call and a Western Union visit. Then there's the historical you walk through, oh, Arusha hotel, you know your place, little temple, little church you happened in and now with it, the bless-ed reverence of the garden and the history come past to you, to this, this passing of the church because of the commitment and the work and that spark from the brow you know not whence it comes, but here and loved and waited for and a pleasure unlike any other. A blue to make the sky cower and here with it, hmmm, I'll leave it at that.

Your father paid for the whole trip with the Texan. From the first time at the first pump when the bill was in the hundreds and then thousands because of the fuel bladder on deck that took a thousand gallons and the oil drums you bounced your head off of with the fish that blew you down the ladder with the drag screwed down too tight and how you still stuck it. Landed on your head and bounced off the drums with two racoon eyes the next day and all that bless-ed money to keep a Texan homeward bound, flat-broke and needing my father and sure of it, that he's doing it for the Texan, the boatlift thing and it just might still be story you drummed up in your sleep to keep your kid on the way seeing how it really was. What got you here, and what will get him somewhere, all these goddamn trinkets and heirlooms we leave our kids to be alright with it. The shit changing so quick, no one can keep it down. Madrid, if you're lucky will still be there and you can start with that, I trust the Spanish still, the Italians not one iota, the Greeks forget it. There're things to be learned. He will have to go out into it, just as you, just as your father and make something of himself. There's no stopping once it's started, it's the bush, and the ocean of green grass, the no Whit, no shit given grass that has you wracked with it, all this come to this shit, after a two decade long *whoop* of living that had you forget what it was. And what you'd left and what you had to put back to get it. It wasn't in the cities and it wasn't in the books and you'd found a smidgen of it in the water and on the water and now this.

The little rolling numbers on the dial of the pump and Pa just pulled out that old style *billetera* and paid the man and did the same for the guy at the bar that wanted to see his family, dropped like 5 thousand so a man can get back to his island and his wife and his kids and now you. Trying even more with all the young people you come across, so maybe 10,000 shillings is too much for bringing coffee and maybe 1,000,000 is too much for

Keto for spotting the cats and waking up at 6 to get out to the bush. But so what? When has generosity ever been bad? What cockamamie goddamn nonsense have they come up with to explain away being nice with money. You always think back to the largesse of that woman shown to Joyce and how she didn't like money and gave it all away and Joyce ate at the Select or some such place the rest of his life. But didn't he deserve it after *Ulysses* and then the *Wake*? Who decides? Let this traitor to his class decide, what I'm leaving when I'm done is on another scale and I know it, all I have to do is prove it now.

When he made that book in '22 he was still wet behind the ears with it but about to come face to face with it and it's good he made it to Europe and even better that his second book was a send-off to Anderson and more amazing still after almost 100 years, the gem was the first one. Imagine knowing writer-painters like this, good god! It feels more true now that as the empire implodes the first to come undone are the writers, they're either bought in or dumb or too damn moist and tepid to give it a decent go. I'm saying it now, I'm here to fix that. And if there's no Paris and no Joyce and no anyone, I'll do it on my own, remember the windsurf?, to me now there's no difference... and I'm going.

We let them all off at the dock and I'm not sure if they paid my father and the Texan, but the women slept or tried to and the small children stayed put in their mothers' laps. It's a beautiful thing to see still today the way small children can get like ferrets in the hollow of their mother's dresses and how they blow cool air on their children's heads and lull and *shush* them to sleep. It wasn't a bad rocking to the boat and came over our beam and she was weighted down enough with the diesel and the load that it was the most comfy she'd ever been on a crossing. Pa and the Texan were smoking cigars up top that some of the ladies had brought with them and they were happy even if they weren't doing it for the money.

We scratched in at daybreak and I don't remember much about the dock or the way they all got off. All I do remember is pedaling every day to Mallory and staying on the pier and watching them sail past on the shrimpers all over the rigging and topsides. It's the same pier he fished on when they were waiting for the Roadster on order and they got waylaid for a good two weeks and finally fell for the place. It might have been the tarpon from that very dock. Remember this was only a trout fisherman and someone who had seen something from a pier from Spain that might have been the run of tuna that come into the Mediterranean for the *almadraba* when the men pull the flat net taut between the boats and chant and gaff the monsters and walk amongst the thrashing beached tuna swimming sideways up to the nets to their death. All the rest is conjecture, it seems all this beautiful serendipity to his life that wherever he went he just completely took on the place and took it to the level it needed taking. Maybe the only time it was in the stars was the first safari and the Africa bit for having Roosevelt's poor little book about adventure. It's hard not to go to town on something like this since the starry-eyed nonsense of youth is shining through so heavily, but heavy lids I guess, when coming across this stuff and maybe a little taste of the Midwest coming through and just what his true personality was. In any case, a good strong youthful man set out on it, a *prodigio* of us when it comes to meeting the right people at the right time and extracting something: women, friends, painters and writers.

I'm trying to get since yesterday someone at the front desk to open the ledger before I leave tomorrow for Manyara and give it its proper due. The Old Arusha hotel has the sign-in book under lock and key opened to page 206 which happens to be 1936, if you go back to '33 you just might get a peek at his name or Pauline's and further back Roosevelt's.

It's strange shit to be stuck with after your father dies and you got that way over his shit, still have the habit of carrying around the dog tag sans chain. And you'll rub it every year and just look deep into it and think about his neck and the sweat and the flying and the P48's or something, you can't remember the model and you're too lazy about the warshit to even care. Just the heroics of that lazed month on the sea when everything just went plum-right and you can almost taste the sweet plum you had out there and what it's like to have fresh fruit at sea when it's been weeks since you've seen anything like a market.

What are the odds you just did a random booking on a country you didn't even intend to fly into on the mobile app of Marriott Bonvoy and then get this; the place he stayed and maybe the balcony too where you've been working like a dog since you finished the last book over in Unguja watching the dhows sail from the roof-restaurant? Does it get any better? Is it dreaming? Or is it the spookiness at a distance that old Einstein couldn't get, some absolute strangeness where you prefigure out of the sky the strangeness of your father's death with a bright yellow tennis ball. This stuff is not supposed to happen and does and we're struck with some antediluvian trust in cause and effect and that the real connective tissue is another, where it's all wired in some strange way and known and repeating and never dying, with ghosts come visit us from our past that is a present. I know it's too dumb to write about so I don't try, I just tend to become bemused a little and let it. Just let it and lean back and think of the grass, if you want it bad enough, though, it seems like that sometimes is enough and all these wraiths just lean in and move the pen for you or hover over you and tap the knuckles on your fingers for the chromebook. And I just let it, Mr. Miller, I owe you too a little here, so *muah*!

My albino girl with the sick auntie brought me the concoction I love, it looks like watermelon but she spikes it with a little orange and papaya and a squirt of lemon and it's as good as Mama's, and I love it. For breakfast, yellow peppers and sharp cheese in an omelet and a healthy dose of bacon, I've given up trying to live a long time so I'm back to the bacon but no banana bread, just toast and one boiled egg, and a slice of green melon and pineapple unless it's sour, I haven't tried it yet.

When you went back to the Keys and drove around a little you happened upon the back streets and felt it, that vague recollection of having been there before and the houses felt familiar, the dead people's place, a small cemetery you must have pedaled into twenty times to remember it this way and the square when you come to it from a special way which must have been the way you took it... See, there must be something to all this, from walking into the bookstore in Hyde park near McDill to the trip to the Keys and off the coast of Cuba with the wish to help out for the boatlift to being struck with it and having no choice and no hope. That all those damn good years in México after you promised yourself yours would get done before his and was and happened on a little portable red Olivetti in a bungalow every morning waiting for her to get her papers ready to head out into it and make a life. It was some vague New York thing you wanted because of your writing and her modeling and then you stayed in México and couldn't get away from the need of it, to do it and make sure it gets done and nothing doing. Just nothing doing, it'd take years more of reading and working at it until your daughter came alone. Not even Lola with the gift of the other manual and how you sat there and nothing. Even built the house with the same portico and fished a whole hell of a lot and had your own boat you didn't really want, another strange circumstance that had to do with the death of your grandmother and a strange unpaid debt to your bro that got resolved with buying his Whaler and then you moved up after seeing the Rybovich in the fishing book from Borders.

It's hard to get so taken with boats when it was a long lost dream you had with your father. All the old conversations came back where he promised the farm on Vieques and the boat to go with it. It all came from that blasted trip you took with him and it buried deep in your psyche when he died and it took your grandma, his mother, dying to flush it out and the weird boat thing and then it just took off and took on a life of its own and you were right in the middle of it. You didn't even wait a day or fish a day in PR after the sale and the refitting of the hydraulic hoses for the steering. You still remember that day on the lift with the hatches up and going over everything and then just taking off with your crew who happened to be Mingi and Petraca. That's what you and your uncle called them and you won't deign to give them their real names, there was a little nastiness on their part to a falling out after the Mayagüez tourney. Before that they had been good except for one of them that worked the new name on the boat in urethane demanding some cash to go fish the DR with us. It was a strange demand this late in the game, purposeful it seemed, the night before leaving and the kid just needed cash to blow off steam in the DR with the ladies.

How do you blame him after a bad marriage and the craziness of drinking in the morning with a cooler in the trunk of his Accord and going through half a case of metralla every day which is our soft pilsner that's as light a beer as you can drink in the tropics.

And so we fished and had a hell of time and I met Lola who I would stay on with in the DR and help raise her family and those first 7 years without a car were the best years you'd ever had, some throwback to what your father promised you and you were giving yourself now that you were a man. It took México and getting the soft shit out of your blood towards women, having your heart unforgivably broken and getting through it to learn your own worth. I like to think it was the boat and the ocean and being all day out there, sometimes for 22 days straight, with the boys, far away from women and all the nasty shit they can put you through if you love them too much.

The reason for the tails and the leg shivering and foot stomping in the bush is the flies. You learn this by carefully watching them. At first when we had lunch with the three hartebeest that stood immobile for an hour just far enough away I wasn't sure of the leg stomping, I thought maybe some nervous tic like with the big female helefump pawing the ground from PTSD or divining for water. What it really was when you got even closer to another hartebeest is an even smaller fly that freckles their whole leg and they stomp the plague off with this periodic shiver and stamp on the ground. It's what all those blasted docs don't show you, the real Africa with all the beautiful details. You were even getting to be a better version of yourself through it all, more observant, quieter, watchful and acceding.

There's always demands in the morning, yours, that it be 6 sharp, that the route be this and the game road you want to be on this or that one when the part of the bush that's most rewarding is the adaptive part: to the rains, and the roads and the general lay of the game the day you drive into it. Had you gotten unnecessarily crazy with your demands of the Kopje in the west you'd have gotten stuck in the muck and slept in the bush, for the desolation and the lack of other drivers that could have rescued you. Instead you went east and finally found your own cats in a tree and then the cheetah, two dens with cubs, tally at the end of the day was 7 cheetah and about 11 lion. Who had a better day? No one.

And there you have it, you didn't get piss-poor angry at Keto for being stubborn about taking you through the sludge out east to the far-off Kopje, you just said, "No" and made it clear and he learned something, damnit!, to not push it. A car with no 4WD and no lockers for the mud and he listened and you changed up and made it out to a second choice that you had devised while thinking the day through. Maybe it was just sweet old age coming down on you like a fresh rain now at 51, or maybe like you're saying you'd come down with it, the bush in your blood, just like the sea those 7 years you fished it straight and now it was just a carryover. All those summers hunting behind Rocky Point with the guns and the rods on the docks and now it was coming full circle and you were good with it, just the tracking and the behavior of them to fill you in. Where before it had been about braining those poor birds in the pine forest now it was about watching and you were good with it.

It's a gentle reprieve when you finally get it. It's got to be this way with everyone. Just a gentle sloughing of the rage, and the loss and the wrongs suffered and now you're just okay with it and let the young guns take it on.

You wish you were at the Serena Ngorongoro lodge instead of Manyara but your mind had done some fancy conflating of the two places where you had a lake levitating on the crater and there was no way to undo this confabulation; either the lake had to go or the crater just became the outright cliff, either way all that mattered was the beautiful blue kudu in the early light and this had happened over Ngorongoro but there was no lake, your mind had just done that to prettify the whole damn thing and there was no undoing what's been done in the writing gig. Goddamn, leave it at 'there was no lake.' It's not easy with the two pulls like tides trying to get down what your mind and the natural rhythm demands with the gently tapping of the djinn on your shoulder to make it concise and metered and like the writing you admire, so be it, just put in the half-thoughts and let it stand as some journalese that goes easy down the gullet with none of the sacrosanct preciousness of fiction, you'd even listed the damn thing when you did the cover art under nonfiction so it had to stand the test of it, or be damned.

I can feel the excitement of tomorrow come on in the writing, it's like the night before a big day in Puerto or the early mornings of the right moon at the end of October before you go out to Macao. You've made one demand of yourself that, because of the damn chromebook, means I need an internet connection, and it's to write like Van Gogh did in the fields, but in the bush. It's about as excited as you can get about writing, which is to make all these animals with their flies and their strange moody ways come to life before your eyes with color and sound and smell and everything in between. You told your mother about the smell of the elephants and how you can smell them long before you hear them gently crashing through the bush or the tearing from when they eat. You said, "old wet rugs laid in the sun in the morning, bad, they smell bad," and it's not their dung, and their tails are weird black heart-shaped dongs but not the sound, the clapper. You've seen some without the ends of their tails from lions usually or some other animal that tears it off when they're young.

It's going to be good to get real writing done in the place that matters. In the absolute thick of it; Manyara is a funny park because of how pushed up it is against the wall of the cliff. There's only room for one game road once you get past the bullshit of the beginning with the picnic tables and a gentle alluvial plain if you can call it that, where the river makes good deadfall from the thickets of trees that bare themselves in the tides the hippos walk through. It's just enough space for a couple elephants to meander through and the zebra are completely unspooked by the cars and nothing like the Serengeti ones that may never have seen people and show every ounce of it from the stop and look sauntering they do when in single file they follow these long processions that can be barely captured by my phone and it's a beautiful thing to see if I had a Leica to capture it, the very and absolute gentle line they make as they follow their trails through the grass going from right of screen to center and curving around and across the screen to eventually cross front and center where my boy can clearly see their beautiful black stripes. Some are reddish, almost ochre, usually young ones and some have heavy black on their withers through their flanks to the place on the topi where they get that strange blue birthmark. When you try to study zebra stripes and you get to the tail and you try to memorize it so you can draw it, anatomy does a funny thing when trying to build stripes on a tail and it settles for T-like intersections, like roadways on a map. Even their heads are distinct, there are no two alike at all, and some have funny-looking dog-like snouts and weird feckless personalities to go with them that have driven them into the maw of a lion that first day you saw the hunt the second time.

~~~~~~~~

I was taking you out to the bush like I said but I couldn't. I tried at the main gate of Manyara to get the doc opened for the chromebook but the damn thing only held it until I got on the cats from the day before. They were beautiful, staring at us and we passed a car that was taking panoramics of the lake from the pass. The pass is unique in the park as it is the only place the main road actually divides the park. I've been able to locate and feel four different parts to the park, a small tropical cloud forest like home where the hornbills will play on the streams and then normal bush which are dryer plains and between these the strangler figs I wrote about in my Spanish books, and so large you can barely see how the trunks have braided their way into an obscenely large tree with pockets of weave that look like dark holes for animals in a beast of a tree, nothing like the smaller Mexican cousins and it was the first time you stopped and talked about trees and Keto seemed to like it. He has this guidebook that I think comes from the government and is good about some animals and better on the trees. Good luck with oryx or the kudu, they just don't bother but we have found civet, genet and honey badger.

And then there's the lake which is unique and then the mahogany forest you drive through towards the end when you get to the other main gate that will take you to Tarangire. I'm not saying there are only four forests, just four types that can pop up repeatedly as you drive through. In the same day, very dry, almost scorched and if in shade, wet and cool, a feeling as strange as anything you've ever felt, almost like different days summing themselves together as you drive through one. The surprise, of course, is the waterfall. It is the only place to have lunch unless you are waiting for cats and just a short drive from the official lunch place with the sulfur springs.

I was like, "Damn, Keto, waterfalls." He looked over a little nonplussed, strange almost as if it wasn't there. I was crazy with the sound of it when we first drove the short grassed greener valley that abutted the cliff. It took me right back to home and I know falling water, just like boat engines, in the distance anywhere.

But the thing is you can't set up for cats in this park but in these two places, the waterfall and the pass because it doesn't seem like the game large enough for the cats will move through these parts without some strange urging.

I'd promised you the bush and like I said the chromebook needed logging in to switch to offline and I missed my chance on the first day and we were as lucky as you could be and had driven up on lion that had just made a kill in the lake at the pass and we were the second car on them and it was late, about 9:30 because we had driven in from Arusha and left at the unholy hour of 7.

I'd grabbed Keto's shoulder when I saw them underneath us as we drove the rocky pass the grader and the digger had cut into the mountain and they were right there not 50 feet from us, quiet, staring, standing in the waist-deep water on the inside of the zebra. The way they dripped each time they took their muzzles out of the water was terrifying and beautiful. These details came later when you sat with them for the whole morning and into the afternoon and the next day when you kept the chromebook open from the main gate and actually got what you were after and then lost it all when you hit some key and it just faded into the damn ether; you should have known better.

So the whole in the bush thing would have to wait until you figured it out, it comes back as snippets and is worked on in the lodge as Keto tries to get the car out of the sand with a busted-up transfer case, you got stuck bad yesterday with a herd of 30 elephant walking through while you tried to get the damn thing out. Only the ranger managed to come get you just as the light was turning blue and you were thinking seriously about it the first time: what it might be like fighting curious cats off from the car in the dead of an almost pitch black night, you were ready though, you'd always been, and the work had made it clear and Keto chose to stay with you when you told him to go after the two cars that had come up on you had tied up and yanked the rear bumper off in a mad-dash of stupidity of leaving too much slack in the strap to chain shit they had rigged up. The running start he had taken was enough to pull a diff out so I guess we were lucky the rear hitch wasn't bolted and just prettified the whole get-up of carrying two spares on the back.

The dumber one and more scared one who had come around because of the deep sand on the Minyara Loop at the dried creek bed got there after the other fellow who was a friend of Keto and was good for the dismasting of the rear of the car. I got into it with him when he didn't want to listen to reason about the falling light and let me understand I might have to go in the car with him to my lodge.

"You're panicking," he said.

I'm like, shit, this fucking dumpling has no idea. He'd put a bit on around the midriff, not that I hadn't, but he was confusing my insistence with incipient fear and I had to tell him.

"Look at me man, do you think I give a shit," I said. You never know with the beard whether all that damn anxiety about your kids and Africa had made a hole large and deep enough to bring on the asymmetry to the general talk of things. I looked like a young Whit with a heat gun held too long to one cheek. If I plucked insistently at night the skin would get red as shit and I could only think about the shit women went through whenever they went for the waxjobs to keep the men excited about the runway. I'd heard nonsense like it's cooler and whatnot, but come on, it can't be that different than what I'd seen yesterday when the baboons stand to with their big old raspberries ass front and center for some calm grooming. We can't be all that different, I'm not judging, just saying.

So I said something about the situation being stupid and the plump driver took it to mean him.

"I'm here for this guy," he said. He meant Keto, as if I deserved being left in the bush. I'm still working out if this is some bullshit racism they got against white people or the more general affront of thinking that every man, woman and child in their car is a dumbass bovine, it could be what I'm always saying about the ravages of tourism and what he lamented would happen to Africa given enough time and market development and he may have been right, but I was working on it and I think I'd found a way to recreate it. It was this: a hunt with the cats from start to finish. By dumb-ass luck we'd driven up on the cats in the lake of Manyara on a fresh zebra, it couldn't have been more than twenty minutes. We knew this from listening to what a driver from another car was telling a passenger when they asked, "When do you think it was?" They'd driven past the game road one and half to two hours ago so we'd been on it at least forty minutes and it made sense, the zebra was open but not eaten and the cats were crazy with rage and one Arab came out through the roof to stand up and film and the young male charged him and crouched and then trotted off to a tree with some bush.

So I tell him, though not exactly, "Get the hell out of here, I don't work for you and take Keto. No one's making me do anything.

You think I'm afraid of spending the night in the bush?" I told him. I wasn't then and only when they left in a huff after taking the chain with them and Keto deciding to stay with me did it come on in the blue light after the main herd had left and we could still hear some tearing and a trunk came up from the dark and pulled the tall branches down, shaking them just like the baboons when they fought in the trees. Then it was different, I started thinking about what we had to fight off the cats with, and if a shovel can even be considered a weapon and my jury came to a resounding fucking no. A little hammer welded from solid steel, a small mini anvil to pipe, that's nothing and one goddamn kitchen knife that would snap in anything if it went in deep enough. I started thinking about all the windows, the ones in the back that slid and the roof, it latched securely with rubber pulls, and what it would be like to fight off cats that came for our smell and the food in the picnic wicker box.

It's a funny thing when you start summing it all up together and then you realize you are fucking scared, you may not give a shit about the dying in a general sense but you start to think about being eaten and fighting if off and then that you must accept it and must let it begin and it's as fucked a thing as there is to think about, because there's nothing fucking clean and clinical about it, you will be going back, carbon by fucking carbon atom back to the ethos of the bush. Suck on that one, goddamn you, I guess it ends in some form of anger to allay the general dread that you're going down in the most antique way there is, that Afar mention of Olduvai peoples that had to truck with it on a daily basis and nothing curried in your mind can get you ready for what it actually is. The zebra brought all this home, it was completely different watching the cats go to town on this submerged striped donkey and they're different cats entirely from the ones lounging in the trees for the tourists or the ones walking languidly by the cars as the photo safari tourists peer over and shutter away. I've done it, I'm not even immune or inured to the damn feeling, it comes on as strong as anything but I have another level from all those years in front of la piedra del Macao and el Faro, 6 thousand hours chasing them through currents and weedlines and bamboo roots and just knowing the general outlay of the canyons on the right tides and when to be there.

My boys from the early tourneys can attest to this fact, I put them on the fish from scouring one little 2 mile long patch of ocean until they came up. And when they did it was 7 of them, one every fifteen minutes until you're sated with how plentiful and *entregado* they can be when they want it. It means given in and surrendered, coming up to feed and throwing themselves with abandon on the lures, we called them *konas* and it stuck in PR and DR and I don't think I ever used the word *lures* on the boat as I never fished with anyone who spoke English and just one rotating observer from that island out in the middle of nowhere in the Atlantic, I forget what it's called but it sounds like Midway which is in the Pacific. It's where the rich people hide their stuff and it's still British.

Anyway, so when Keto sees sand or something difficult, he goes straight for it and he did nothing less than when he saw the sand in the creekbed. I'd told him to stop that shit from the last time when he wanted to drive out to the west Kopje when we were after the rhino and he'd been insistent and I'd had to get stern on him and only then did he desist. He still failed to understand about taking a line and thinking it out beforehand and to do that you had to study the terrain and that's something he just didn't do. He worried about problems when he was plumb in the middle of them and with sand when you stopped and thought about things you were already stuck, especially with a busted transfer case.

So he did the same thing with the sand in the Minyara Loop and I was up through the roof thinking about it and looking at the sand deciding if it was even worth it and by then it was too late. He had stopped and already started spinning with the limited diff when what you needed was low pressure and locking hubs for this shit, moreso when you shouldn't be getting out of the car and kneeling and locking hubs in the bush with all the cats and the elephant.

But that was yesterday, today I'm at the lodge going ham on the chromebook trying to get all of three days down in the jumble of how it falls back and my real intention was some line drawing in the bush and it turned out to be this petite drama about getting stuck and riffing on the shit about tourism and some latent strange shit that happens between the drivers and their apparent understanding of the idiocy of their charges. For what it's worth, it's not that bad going over it and the rehash, but what I was really after was the feeling of the bush and the luck of having finally after 14 days in it to come upon a kill, a fresh one, with some very angry cats and the beauty of the lake and that it was so strange being in the water and having the elevation to look down on it.

There were 7 cats, two youngsters, a full-bodied male without mane and the rest females. One with a collar for tracking and a shy female and the lead who was as calm a cat I have ever seen given all the hysterics of the others of having felt threatened on their kill and being truly wild cats in the bush who probably don't see a lot of people in a park like Manyara.

The waiter just asked me as I walked down to the hut they call the palapa gazebo down beneath the pool about my starch.

"Just need to ask about your starch."

And I'm trying to figure out what the hell, and it's about the rice or potatoes, it's the beautiful thing about Africa, what they do to the language where when we hear it, we're like, "Okay, it can be new, it can be said right", and starts standing with an utter dignity. And isn't that what Pound was getting at when it came to disuse and vague withering notions of truth when stretched so thin nothing means nothing anymore? Isn't that what I'm supposed to be doing here and trying, the Sisyphean feat of raising from the dead that which is hell bent on staying dead in an empire?

~~~~~~~

After two weeks in the bush and a sleep from 7:30 to 10:30 at the Arusha hotel I made the worst question I could have asked of the kind girl who told me about her sick mother.

"She passed away," she said.

What do you say, really? I'd been thinking a lot in the bush about my own mother's passing and whether I would take it and how and it just came over me, the whole bullshit of death, the real bullshit, the sudden knowing like curtains blowing that it's gone and passing through and you will continue, you may, you just may and breakfast will decide it and then lunch and then whether you can sleep and if you can't you must decide and how and for how long and make all the arrangements. Go see what you always wanted to, there's a fellow selfied, last shot at the Grand Canyon just before and it's a beatific smile, just letting you know, a last act of kindness, it's not this world, it's beautiful and it's not sadness, just no more, not for me, it's at the heart of all our mysteries and you will contend with it, like it or not, some day, and you can respect that, but it's the hardest thing. The very kind... I shall not say it but eventually, yes, them too.

Do it, do it now, but the animals kept you, it was a good trip, a very very good trip. Leopard, cheetah, and many lion. Totals are, thus far, 1 leopard, two cheetah, at least 40 unique lion. Overall, 5 leopard, 11 cheetah, and well over a 100 lion. But the real stuff now, on this trip at least 7 hunts, and one first meeting between father and cubs. What more can you hope for?

I'm not saying that this is it, it isn't. No sacrilege to it, but I've found something, slightly foolish, and selfish and beautiful and pure. It's the shoulders of a female cat as she takes the grass on and chooses her line. The last one happened not 10 minutes before we had to drive to the main gate at Naabi.

We'd set up on the cats the day before and thought them two separate prides. The furthest up the hill was a male, two females and three youngsters. The youngsters, we'd taken to calling them that, for their adolescence and size, they were almost the size of a full cat but with nothing of the experience and still completely reliant on mother for the hunt, or sisters, whichever be the setup for the hunt that day.

Down the hill at about 250 yards and near a river were two females sunning on the road near a creek with the dark green bush grass the cats love. We'd found the cats again early, around 7 after the hour drive to the plains. You pass these island rocks and the road changes from red sand to packed main road gravel to black earth, slippery as hell with the LandCruiser going crazy in the ruts if there's a little curve to it. Coming out the night before we got lucky with the patchy rain that slicks down the road. The only thing is neither Keto or me gives a shit about spending it in the bush so it's likely a reprieve to have to and will settle some matter for him whether

I'm really as unafraid as I say I am. It's nothing I want to test but I'm okay with it and he has that hellbent drive to adventure at any cost that makes me think he may be okay with it too. It's that risky number they give us when doing demographics that account for our slightly higher birth rate from 50/50. We kill ourselves because of it and the mother of my daughter *me reclamó* when paddling out at Puerto on an 8 foot day just to swim it with our Vipers. Some shit about, 'How could she trust me, if I take these risks and put her in this predicament?' We did get a full throttling on the swim in. You have to time it too perfectly to get in through the inside and she started panicking and I followed her–she didn't really give me a choice and we took them all on the head. I'd been able to hold her for the first one and swam to her for the second one but the wave ripped her out of my hands and I was even trying to leglock her underwater with my ankles crossed to not lose her in the absolute wrath of it that feels like your falling to thump hard on the sand and then everything gets blown every which way and she came loose. It may be why I don't see my daughter, some cat shit, where they don't let them see you until you're deemed fit.

So, we were the first ones on the last morning on the cats and they'd moved out into a field and the first thing we saw was their termite hill manes popping out of the gold grass. We both knew and both glassed them and it was the two males headlocked in pantomime of coinage, perfectly crossed, perfectly looking two separate ways and a dihedral of symmetry to make you cry if you're a cat lover which we're not.

We tried counting them but there's no counting in the grass when it's that tall at that distance, something like a 100 and a quarter yards and it was just the typical early morning relaxing after a night feeding. We'd thought the two prides separate the day before and I was the first one to say "one pride", but then we agreed it wasn't until we got the count and were able to see the cats one by one. All 13 of them or so we thought, more started appearing when they did the walk down to the creek to drink and sun. If you've never seen a cat drink, it's something. I'm guessing no less than 5 solid minutes. No pauses, just drinking, a slow lapping almost as delicate as a housecat and careful about the mud in the puddles on the outer edges the wildebeest make. When full, a gentle trundle off and to lay it out on the mound of black earth under a tree.

There is something about the forearms of a cat up close, it's as if they've been lifting, the veins draw out the fur not just on their legs but all over their backs and they're gentle African rivers under the golden fur. A long line crosshatches the ribs, a long lean muscle, that in us, if we swim gives us the wings on our backs the women love, triangles us and gives us arch and perfect form, my father said it, best bodies, swimmers and ballet dancers. Momma wouldn't have it, so I never danced, but he said Nureyev got all the ladies and it was important to Dad that I get all the girls, said it on the boat ride up to The Keys after sideskipping Mariel, "*Arranca bloomer.*" He really wanted it for me, after debating with the captain what a good boy was, they agreed that getting the girls was the holiest Grail and so I ended up in a roller rink at 9 with a 15 year old that had no clue of my age watching her halter shake as luscious as Bisset in The Deep as she fell to her knees and me holding her hands on the canted wooden floor. No other first times, son.

They sunned most of the hottest part of the day. We stayed with them all of the morning and Keto had put the car up on a mound of grass off to the part of the road that you could drive off. Sometimes, not very often you could end up in a warthog hole, so you had to be careful and I always walked to the back and stood on the refrigerator between the last row of seats through the roof and guided him back. This time we found good earth and parked it and had breakfast, Keto passed me his egg and I asked for the salt. Nothing doing, only one morning out of 6 did I get a packet but the eggs, hard boiled, were so good they didn't need it. I'd learned to trust the sallow colored yolks more, some even tending to a greenish death that scared the shit out of me with getting something like salmonella. But they were all good and some were even as good as a semi-wild home chicken like in Vieques or the DR when you'd put your hand under them and pull them out still warm if the chicken let it. Others and you had to hunt them down, one time she'd been gone for weeks and I found her under the wasp bush with a clutch of 15. None with chicks, all beautiful but fallow, dead with lack of gallo and she kept to them and we thought it the Holy Grail after so long, but they were green inside and tasted funny. So much for the coop and locking it every night; after that they all went up the mango tree and it's a pure pleasure at dusk to watch them staring up and then go. It's something I don't know why I like, some ancient timekeeping that seems just right.

I'd been wanting one last hunt so we talked about it and Keto mentioned the Gol and I wanted to drive through it. There's no other perfect way to get into or out of the Serengeti. It's an open grassland with elephants down by the black earth and "black rock", they call it, and kopjes and then the full Gol which is like a deadly dream that lures you into it where we found all the cheetah that day and drove like hell from island to island until we were well south of Naabi and then ultimately outside the park and no way back but a half-day's walk if the hyena didn't get you. I'd been joking with the cook back at the lodge about the 'fisi' and throwing the bones to them outside the low gate around the fire where I had dinner once it got dark after we got back. One word at a time Swahili and then you begin to have it and then you hear it as the drivers talk about the day to each other as they take their charges on the humdrum roll. For us it wasn't, it just wasn't, it'd taken two solid weeks of laying my foot down that I wasn't a tourist and then I finally went gently into my good night of not imposing myself anymore and still getting what I wanted out of it, which were the hunts.

This day it was to get them to do it. The cats, I'd learned, just didn't like to hunt until they did. If that meant waiting all day in a sleep for something to walk over you then that's what you did, waited and slept and popped your head up every so often. It's the most beautiful sight, the neck of a lion and its arch and the short nose, the rounded black ears and if the light is right a perfect bust over the grass at any distance when glassing.

I'm still trying to get the key to the locked case of the sign-in ledger, goddamn that glassed cabinet and its draw, I even tipped the front desk 20,000 shillings and then pouted it out. And to look cool, said later, all for one signature around the 26th of December 1933 or '36, I'm forgetting years now. There's these two worlds, the backend and the now of this thing called Africa. It's holy when you're out in it and then they blast *You're so vain* on the balcony as I do this, between looking up Shipman or the *West with the Night* and sending a copy to my daughter I have to go back to the light and the yellow binoculars on the roof of the LandCruiser and then the thoughts of my son and what he's missing and how I could teach him about the look of the cats and how what I'm after is so ephemeral and somewhere between sadness and original loss, that it might be biblical and you have ideas for stories of all your friends from a to z and what they meant to you and how all books should start with our friends, it's the first thing we find and then we lose, it's earlier than love and cuts deeper and stays longer. Mine did. I'd call him Randy and talk about the bad shoulder from pee-wee but I'll save that, it's a damn good story when it gets to the girl and how she messes him up for good and how he almost lost it all–true tragedy. But for now the cats.

"My boy," I'd tell him, "watch: you see how they get up and stare at the herd from their sleep? They're hunting, not sleeping, the rest is a strategy." This day they slept all morning and then they walked off to the creek and the cars came and then we went and we waited. While they were all taking pictures and the cats were right next to us and I was watching the notched ear on one and her stare that I didn't trust and the old collared female with her broken rivers of vein on her fallen and withered back as she walked past and Keto rolled up the window and I didn't want him to, I was watching a young female as she walked off and told him.

"It's a hunt."

"Yes," he said.

"I'm sure of it."

"Yes."

You get these short real answers when you're watching something, really watching something like cat go out into the grass, far from her pride and do it.

And she was off with all the decision and decisiveness of probably not having eaten last night with the good moon, made to eat last and now hungry with it and committed and walking, steady and forthright and with an ear and a plumb-line sight for the wildebeest and a green monticule she will start from. Here, she begins, it's a slow uphill so the wildebeest cannot see her and besides, the others are going off slowly and it's a wild guess at this point glassing which it will be, but I guess the one with its back to me and only at the end do I learn that I'm right.

All the tourists in the three cars parked side-saddle to the cat on the black earth are mesmerized with the cub that comes from between the cars and another cat walks past, the old collared female and it's three now, four if you count the cub, ear-notched, old lady and beautiful forearms and cubster who is small and just yesterday met his father for the first time—another story entire but part of this one. So, the fourth car from the out-west lodge with the big cameras stops and puts the three cars between them and the cats and manages in the space we've left to telescope out those big-ass lenses. It's kind of foolish, moreso with the Swahili driver with a camo one but so it goes. It must be something with the booking, I kind of like the honesty of my $29.99 getup, cell held always in panoramic, the way the Euros do and all the people here for the first time. It must be some type of daft snobbery where it's indicated with what you've spent how serious you are about the animals. But I'll bet I do it better with what I've got, it's not a hunt when I see what they're after, the hyper-pixelated close-up–*THE CAT*. You can't really argue with that, with what all stem myopia has done to us, it's probably the nature shows and the fetichism of between your legs staring in the marital quarters, hell I don't know and I don't have time for it–she's made her way deep into the nubbin of grass that separates her from the wildebeest with his back to us. I only know from the shape of his horns, it's all I can see and the fact he doesn't tilt his head to eat, just a gentle swaying pendulous look that only quarters his head. So I'm sure of it, sitting with his legs under his side just taking in the morning. Keto is trying his hardest to give a shit, but I can tell finally there is no shit to give, he thinks because I'm glassing that I don't notice that he's facebooking and crazed with the notification, never silent to ping him to, an attention grabbing salute to his lap he swears I don't notice but I'm with him in his not giving a shit, 'cause I don't either. This is too good, the cat's been down a long time, making her final approach, and I'm blind to all of it until she does jump it's back and it's a half-assed jump and she slides off and the thing goes running off and all the other game stands to, 4 zebra are stock-still, the faces look black from the yards between us and it's time to go, there will be no more hunt today, there isn't enough game to set up and the cat is standing, just staring at what could have been as it runs off. And somehow I managed one last hunt in the last minutes before noon and the two safe hours we need to head towards the main gate of Naabi, one and half for travel and half for the bullshit of anything going wrong with the car. Two is our checkout time and this is a religious by the double dot, number behind the colon better get it right or pay another day's lodge and rec fee to Tanapa to overnight again which I'd never mind. How can you?, it's the Serengeti and every day a gift in this wonderland.

I didn't even know what to make of it when I first got here, I'd been hell bent on Nairobi for just plain lack of knowing any other name to Africa and where to begin. I guess it was the airport, it might have something to do with where he started and stayed on for his second safari, whatever it was, Stone Town decided it for me, mine was a strange way of traveling where I got on *FlightConnections* and just punched in my present city and saw where the vagaries of *destinos* took me, if it looked like a good city, I went. Istanbul was good with Zanzibar and Zanzibar was good with Arusha. And so it went and I ended up here and loved the hell out of it, didn't even know about the Serengeti or that he stayed at the same hotel and don't remember reading when I did about Manyara or Babati or any of it, it's just those kind of trips I went on and it was working out pretty good thus far.

A strong massage yesterday, my first in ten years, sponsored by Doudas and two girls, four oiled Swahili hands starting at the legs and going up to the scalp and the whole thing reeked of *Mountains of the Moon* when he's smoking on the balcony, I don't know where and he's describing how in spite of not having it they're still commendable. He meant good at it, I don't remember what he said, but Burton was trying to insinuate what he wanted his guests to believe. The movie went terribly south with the whole bit about England and getting proper and married and the bullshit with Speck. But you can forgive him this for *Five Easy* and how damn good it was. It was also made good on by *A New World* when she said, "Did you find your Indies, John?" Goddamn, that's stuck a hell of a long time and all adventurers when they come home and ask it, must ask, "Did you, did you really?"

It's the thing about travel and leaving home, you should really be leaving yourself, and for the crazies and the ne'er-do-wells they always manage to leave themselves and if there is any travel to be done, this is where to begin. She asked it and meant it, did you find it outside of love, you Americaño, you, did you really? Really? REALLY? Ask it, ask it now. Have you left ever? Ever? You?

It's a hard one and it has something to do with death and I guess it's why I'm so hard on all the camera-toting windbags going *shick-shick*, they don't know really, you can't photograph the cats until you are the cats. I told my mother last night, trying to explain it to her, you become the cat when you chase it. Get just as lazy and can't, because if you do really fall asleep you won't see that one cat walk off and do the hunt on her own. I won't count, and can't, it's been a lot, somewhere around ten. All of them good, all of them rapturous, some standing up in the car and watching the large male have it get turned and the herd of 6 buffalo come for him and him chasing the creek and the downslope of it to get away and his thick padded trot in the grass as loud as pillows being thumped over your head and the breathing *huff* and head swinging craziness of the buffalo as they snorted past. You'll know it and keep it if you get it, not the camera, no, and I was getting it on my $29.99, swinging the whole thing past, finally breaking up my own fetish for the 13 second Messenger friendly pert short clips for this goddamn real one. That's how you know, when the old mind has to shut off because you're on the ride now and there's no framing and no looking at the camera, you're just swinging your arm in the general direction and alive with it as it happens. Buffalo and lion, *vroom!* past, no breathing and Keto as quiet as he can get, that's how you really know, when there's no fakery in it, he's seen it all and half of it is a gentle con of mimic where he does what you do and after 28 days of it, even you're inured a little to it, all the cat and the animal and it's so good you've become it. I was saying cat, I am cat.

You become what you chase, I'd have to go back to shake-a-spear for it, to see what he has to say. He's no Maasai though, my city Maasai at the mobile camp only grabs it and escorts you to the zippered flap at night, at day, be damned you, there's no cats. You got angry at first with it, the presumptiveness that no animal walks in the last of the dawn as the plain takes light, but they do, but there's no use getting angry out here, live or die, it doesn't really matter, the only way to enjoy this is to ride it and just let it, I mean it, just let it.

And I have, and I'm good for it, a lot better than I was before I got here. The writing is going, it's the best I can hope for and I think if you ever do leave all this and give it a go, remember this: before you're read and well before you're sung, it should be you, any halting or tepid resonance in the echo chamber that has you asking, 'How so-and-so would have…' and you haven't left, it's a voyage of you and that's why we pay passage and it's the true ship we're on. Remember that, young Huck, or you, you out there, it's you I write to, maybe bereft, maybe pining for it, wanting it so bad you get lost in it at first glance, and then you sink deep into it, the morass of the words and then you're alive in it and wanting it so bad you might gallivant some half-assed mongrel

attempt to live it, do like I did and get your ass to
México right after waiting a month for the copy to come
in hardback to Cronopios when it was still on I forget the
name of the street in the old city, near the park where
Jessie pissed standing up and the old man with your
father's name and the shock of white hair made paper
flowers and serenaded Jessie after she'd wiped with the
napkin she always carried for these drinking fests and
how you were all there, all your good friends, now lost
to the fog of time and with exits of lonesome giving in to
the differences, some wrathful yet quiet, the way all
good friendships end in the harrowing of years. Good
god.

Long before you're read and sung you will have
this, the time alone and the deliciousness of it, long
languid afternoons and mornings in your hotels, on your
balcony in Arusha, on your boat when you get it back;
you should have never sold it and just checked the
Rybovich registry, #50 and she's still yours even though
you sold her, like a woman who still loves you in the
arms of another, you know it, kid, you just know it. It
happened with the mother of your girl, little ocean of us
we put in this together, a thousand words, all contained
in one now. Hunt others, did you? And now back to this
and you can't forget that look she gave you at the Santa
Fe, half turning in the light, this no bullshit narrative, but
true, wanted death, and dying, love has its ways. The
Tehuana in her, famed and fabled matriarchy rising in

her blood like a wash, like a gouache as they sponge the walls with chestnut and caramel and mamey as they say in the DR, hard gristled, edgy color with proof of hand and reminded of it now, here, the caves, always the caves, like you told your mother, Chauvet, and the lion, the real lion, the arc of neck and pouted snout and the look, only gotten from the grass and the half km stare at the game and then you know, hunter, hunter of you, and they were to far gone, maybe an herb, maybe psilocybin, whatever had them ignoring themselves and capitulating entire to the animal, gave it, gave it you.

The trip went like this, it's time to clear the fog up: two short trips of three days, Manyara and Tarangire followed by a longer one, pure Serengeti and lucky to get it as good as we did, 6 holy days… You'll see what I mean later, I mean holy as industrial holy, that's as much as a reprieve as I can give until I can give it in full. Oh hell, I'll give it now, it was toward the backend of the trip, I'd booked the tent for six nights with Doudas and glad of it, I missed the fisi howling, almost cooing in the dark if they were far off enough. One even managed to get under the wood floor of the stanchions on which the tent and me above it slept, I didn't mind at all and seemed to sleep better with it; the only time I did spook was with a lion and his hoot and, I swore, the footsteps outside the door and woke ramrod up and thought, and turned on the bed light and looked over at the wooden bathroom door and thought it, a last stand in there and

I'll break the mirror and tear through the roof and get up on the guide that holds the whole roof on roof up and just scramble over the top of the tent onto another and gamble with jumping off and the other cats surely around outside. This is the nonsense a mind goes through when thinking about saving itself, until I said to hell with it and went back to sleep in the Serengeti.

We were up early, I set two alarms and always sleep through the first at 5:30, the second if I'm sleeping deeply enough at 5:35 feels like right away, if I'm already up with the expectation of what the new day brings I usually just get up and hit dismiss so it doesn't bug me while I'm getting the water warm. It's scalding hot if you let it and you have to be careful but I go full hot, then off, then full cold and it works out good with what's left in the tubes to not have to fuck with it too much beyond that. I just need enough water to get the road out of my hair, I'm always too tired to shower before I get to bed and I've made a habit of sleeping grungy, *mugroso* I like to think and don't give a fuck. I like not giving too much of a fuck in the bush, it helps with what I smell like and I like it; if you smell too good in the bush it's a putoff and I can always smell all the other safari cars with the lather and the soap and the godawful shampoo fragrance–you have to try to meld at some point, don't you?

Most don't and I'm the road in this one. Keto's good too, not too much of anything and there's literally no smell to us in the car, all the torn up mud and dust from the wheel wells to the backend helps–you're trying to get the bush into the bush, I don't really think the cats mind, but I do.

Anyway, I pack everything in the green Dakine with the chromebook and the undershirt, I will use the same black Rustler jeans and the linen blue shirt my son's grandmother gave me, if it's chilly I'll just go undershirt, another gift, a thermal black undershirt that is good-warm and nothing against the tsetse flies, I'd thought them horseflies and probably have the sleeping sickness by now for having let them bite me through and through to smack them good until I went full Buddhist and just shooed them away. We'd learned to keep the LandCruiser tight at all the seals and go out into it with a hermetic seal and hope for the best, some always did come in and with the switched-for-car the glass slides back against itself and the flies get stuck between the panes and the buzzing drives you crazy until you swore you would switch cars and you waited for the fixed up one to be done and driven in from Arusha to Manyara and which you are now heading out in with the wicker lunch box and your slung backpack and the mornings from the staff and the: "How did you sleep?", and all the goddamn protocol you've taken as normal and such a far remove from what you grew up in that the shock wears off, but slowly.

It's dark, the light won't begin to come up until 6 sharp.

"I heard cats," Keto says.

"Me too," you tell him.

"What time?" I ask after the driving pause.

"Late."

They never coincide and it's best to not go into it. We each have our own cats and I think we both know they don't come through the camp so there's no use trying to create unnecessary expectation to the day with the full tourist bullshit, and he's not pulling it anyway. It's good, you like it that way, Keto's convinced he can hear cats from 16 km away, I stick with the wiki fundamentals of half that, but I have heard the far-off ones once and they're hard to hear and I imagine myself a whale with the low reverberating hum coming across the Atlantic while I cradle the bottom in my Spanish book and then I become the helefump and imagine the ultrasound rumblings through the ears of my feet and get way too technical and science savvy to give too much of a shit and stick with the real bush we're driving out into.

They're there on the road when we turn out onto it, with just enough light to see them, only Keto can, his eyes are better. Two big males, I won't see just how big until later when we get them in the better light, we see just enough of them crossing the road when they see us to go north across the rising sun. It's not a true rising just the gunmetal blue of early morn, well before the ribald glee of the orange light and succulently dark and bad enough to get spooked about taking the Turner game roads in, which we do.

We have three of them and this is the first true morning in the Serengeti. 6 days of it and here we are with two toughs this early and this lucky, before 6 to start with it and the best in Keto comes out and he picks it exactly on the second try, the second game road that is.

He finds them first, the light is good by now, full day, what the photogs love when they take the girls to the beach to film the golden light and they cross again and they have the look; I get the full scope of their size now, big brothers, it's what we end up calling them: the brothers, Emil and Aloysha, I think, not from the book but from real people I knew growing up, one with a torn scalp re-sown after a mauling by a car and the kid was good. These were the bohemian friends my father had and they always had crazy names for their kids, Sun, Lady, all kinds of literary shit it's best not to go into, and here I am doing the same for my kids, I don't know if the copyright nonsense will let me give you their real ones, let's just say I went ham and started with the oldest tropes of water and original traveler.

So the brothers cross against the light into a field and it's strange how quick we got it but they spot two buffalo and they trot off quick, almost a steadfast run and then they spot one. The grass is light green and there's good trees in these hills. The terrain behind the camp is rolling hill with good cover and solid bush, we're paralleling a creek which isn't dry but does make it steep and the lion the buffalo decide to chase is heading down to it. Later, I'd call it a hunt, but now it seems like a retreat. Some huffing had alerted a herd of 5 from out of the long shade of a short tree and they'd come for the lone buffalo and the chase had started. I'm through the roof with the damned phone but not really paying attention to it. The lion is hightailing it using the car almost, and getting as near as he can as he runs past downhill to the creek and disappears into it with the 6 buffalo after him. The other brother who was flanking is way up the hill and just standing and then it's all over.

Only later did I realize in their retreating it was still a hunt, these buffalo are so big that going full bore down a hill and into a scruffy creek bed with slick rock is a deathtrap if they slip and break a leg–it's how smart big cats are, they're using the natural aggression of the buffalo against themselves and getting them to commit in their rage to propositions of terrain that you can hunt from the back-peddle, I like it, true Sun Tzu stuff and a thinking man's game to watch, almost like taking in a Capablanca gambit, you don't know what you're getting until you're too deep into it, three sacrifices and you're scotched, your wheels up against the rubber and nowhere to go, parked and cannot fly shit.

Anyhow, I was agog with the glory of watching my first male lion hunt. If you think about it and your mind's been all fucked up with watching the nature drivel, it's nothing like that and gloriously so. I'm not going to get too deep into it and spoil it for all you adventurous souls, but if you get out and are lucky enough to get something like this all to yourself and the trees are all around and your deep down a game road, a mobile camp road really, but in the off-season when the camps are empty they become de facto game roads that no one goes down, so you're alone with it and you have to love that, if you go to the central Serengeti where everybody commingles you'll miss this, the glory of being alone with it and maybe just lucky enough to see it in all its trueness. You'll take this with you forever, the light, the look of the animal, the buffalo–I can't say this enough, the buffalo, black headed and bossed with this spread of evil, of deadly evil and tough and husky with the command of themselves and the decision to face it and kill and take it down, this damn lion, while they go, lead by a leader of balls-to courage and to chase it down. These lion are not small and they're two, that's almost a grand of lion, a thousand pound of cat coming toward you, in dervish and unison when they do that death jump on your rump and then turn and paw to hoof get your neck and keep you from running. And take you down.

But they haven't, you want four stories, maybe slightly more of all your friends, they finally feel complete. You'll start with Randy, and move on to Ari and then Gene and then, maybe the others that meant less, even some you didn't like. Randy would go something like this: his shoulder was limp from pee-wee and–I already did this, I need to get to his wit... He made himself as funny as he was ugly from the ghost whiteness and the droopy shoulder. It's what happens when all the nerve and sinew and muscle completely collapse, it looked like an old woman's thigh from having stopped walking, and this was the top of the shoulder and then he had a pretty good one on the other side and he got so funny, the girls started liking being around him. It wasn't the funny ha-ha of jokes but real wit, Ma always said it was his Irish ways and you had to believe it was some sort of gift. But what it really was, was his intelligence. He'd found a goddamn secret about saying it the way it was and everybody loved him for it. He got on good with the upperclassmen and he was a good sailor from his father. We'd windsurfed every afternoon after school if it was blowing, and the trades usually let up by just around 6, so we had two good hours if we ran downstairs and didn't eat and rigged up and carried the boards out quick. The trick was to leave them rigged and just let up on the tension, I still have the feel on the soles of my feet of pulling down on the mast and the boom. Randy's technique was so good, he sailed in the top class, my legs were too spread out and I had a funny way of holding the boom, his technique was spot-on, legs together, very far back and pulling boom back behind his shoulders, there's just a way were it begins to look good and he had it, it'd take me years of thinking it out on the boogie to get it down on the big waves of Puerto, but even with his fucked-up shoulder he was a natural.

The thing was it didn't matter with the girls and Randy was pissed about getting scraps. I had a girl out in Dorado I liked a lot who was thin and had the darkest softest hair and we'd drive out already a little fucked up from smoking and take some vodka and go sit with the girls on the golfcourse and mess around for a couple hours and then drive home.

I was glad he was getting some even if we were only messing around and kissing and grabbing them a little, but it made me happy that he was happy too and I was telling him so on the highway in the jeep.

"She's good, huh?"

"She's alright," he said.

"What do you mean alright, she likes you a lot."

"Dude."

Dude meant a lot of shit but mostly it meant lay off the way he was saying it. It had rained on the way home and then stopped and the road was wet and still a little warm from the sun. It could be so warm it would steam. I'd known from having slept on it, it took till 4 for it to cool down completely. Sleeping on the road is another story I won't get into. The thing was we started sliding and no matter what I did with the wheel there was no way to correct, she just spun any which way. I could keep her going forward with just the bitching fishtail that wouldn't stop and by then we were on the wet grass on the left and she went sideways into the guardrail.

"Dude, what the fuck?" He was pissed.

"I had it."

"You didn't have shit," he said.

"I had it," I said again. I was just happy I'd kept it pointed the going-way forward. I also felt good about going flush into the guardrail. The tires were so wide they were like bumpers on a ship. I kind of like the way she bounced off. We were stopped in the dead silence of the highway with no one on it.

"Gimme a smoke," I said. Shit always got settled with a smoke.

"You didn't have shit and you know it, you're talking out your ass."

"No I had it," I said. The mind is like a fortress. I lit up and passed it. He didn't stick it to his and grabbed the lighter.

"You're so full of shit."

"How was she?"

"Good."

"I didn't see you. Where did you go?"

"To a roof," he said. "You?"

"Stayed on the field."

"Hmm. Next weekend?"

"Yeah," I said. "Let's get the fuck out of here."

We would crash again but worse this time, I flipped it on my side and I never came to until the EMT's brought me back. Randy was good, but my girl lost too much of her pinky and part of her shoulder and they didn't graft and what grew back was weird pink and didn't feel right and then I got sued and Randy's family didn't. I always respected him for that and truly loved his family for having kept the code.

Much later when I snapped my C7 on the sand in Puerto and the MRI said I was damned lucky I lost my two good fingers on my left hand. Then I started thinking about her a lot trying to do things with the damn fingers asleep for over two years. I'm talking dead asleep as if you slept on them and they don't just wake up–it's an annoying feeling you got used to just like your father's death–all things come down eventually.

What fucked up Randy was an ex. I'd snapped out of her on her front lawn when skipping rope and asking her little sister, all of 8, "Who was it that called?" when she went in to get it. This was back with rotary phones, you had to be real careful about dialing if you wanted to sneak a call in without your mother hearing. There's a soft push to the hole in the dial and letting it come back with your finger that gets you a call without all the jingle jangle of those phones. Later Randy got a girl off my girl who had a Jetta with the first phone in a car on the island and it was fancy shit to see that took all day to install in the car and looked like something out of the original *Wall Street* except no one had them. They were jewelers and Randy didn't like her but it kept us together and was a small concession to get the perks of going out together, dating was always a compromise and if he didn't get uppity with it he'd always be okay.

The thing was after I asked, she said the name of my cousin. It was Ponchy and no one on the island had the name so I just hung it up with her and almost three years later he came at me with: "You mind if I date Cass?"

I was like, shit, that's crazy. I liked him asking, but it seemed foolish, we all dated around and everyone was hooking up with everyone and we had a name for it that I think was scraps, but we never said it. I was glad my friends could date my exes, it was almost a town and we liked keeping everyone around, it made the parties and the drinking easier when everyone really knew everyone. My skinny black haired girl was with a future doctor and I was glad and I should have told Randy about her, but I didn't.

He came back to me at the pool one day.

"Man we were doing it," he started, "and she let me do it. God, it was like falling into something. It was dark, man."

It was the strangest shit I'd ever heard and it's hard to believe the bluster when it's conquest talk. I'd never done shit like that, but I'd heard some crazy stories about her and it seemed a little off that he would tell me this about her, she was the first girl I ever loved but I was enough of a badass to cut her off when she went with Ponchy. The streetfighting and the surfing helped and a healthy dose of not give a shit that you could only get from the streets of PR.

I really wanted to ask a lot of questions from not having done anything remotely similar and it just seemed weird but what he was really saying was how deep he'd sunk, he was in love with her and I'd never warned him, never given him the reasons, never told him about my cousin and never about the deeper shit I knew about her mind and what she really wanted, which was to just fuck guys up. She had something special for me and it was a suspicion at first and then a certainty that she was using Randy to get back at me. Her parents had put her in a new all girls school and it's where my new girl went and something had to give in her mind and the war of dating my friends was just something I was ignoring, it was the healthy dose of the streets and learning to not let girl's shit phase you, they could only hurt you if you let them.

Randy fell hard for her and then she dumped him and he got deep into coke and as fucked up as you could get. He was always the best student in the school and had the highest score ever for our school on the SATs. He was a reader, just like me and when we weren't sailing we were reading sci-fi and loving a Piers Anthony series that went on for like 15 books. He liked my mother's fruit shakes and always came up from the 6th floor to my

10th, only his faced the ocean and mine the mountains but we could do whatever we wanted at mine 'cause Mom was never home and always worked late.

I really should have told him, it's a hard thing seeing your friend like that, I even got fucked up with him once so he would feel better, I didn't like the shit and the guys that sold him the shit were shits he wanted to hang out with who always flashed their money at the school and had boats and all the fast girls and Randy was always trying to move up before he wore out his last pair. It was all really about Cass and how she'd left him and nothing was making it better.

He begged me one night to take him to cop some dope at the projects behind the building and we went in his father's company car with him driving, he wanted to buy an unholy amount of dope and a trans walked up on us after we parked.

"¿Cuánto?" she asked.

It's a hard thing to quantify an amount when what he really wanted was a boatload of shit for all this money he had so she just showed her and the bitch put something to his neck right away when he flashed the cash.

This was no dainty trans, these were bitches with balls that'd beat any man up and I grabbed her hand and didn't feel myself getting cut up. I was so fucking worried about his neck and her nicking him good that I just grabbed.

"Reverse, fuck" I said. I almost whispered 'fuck.' I was too worried about his neck and trying to concentrate for him on the fucking lever coming down that one fucking notch.

His hand was trying but the lever wasn't jamming, it was one of those steering column things and he was forgetting the brake, I think, to let it in. Shit seemed like forever and the trans grabbed all the dough and he got it in and we just left.

I was pretty angry at him but I loved him as much as you could love a friend and would do anything for him even if it meant doing shit I didn't believe in just so I knew he was okay. This was a close one.

"Come on man," I said. "You got a smoke?"

"Yeah."

"You alright?" I asked. My hand was fucked up but I didn't feel it yet and I had it closed and then I smoked with it. It was streaked but not dripping.

"I'm good," he said. I wanted it to be a lesson but he'd have to sleep in the stairwell to get this girl out of his blood, all the dope in the world wasn't going to do it. He shipped off a year later when his parents almost gave up on him and he's never been okay with the girls.

The Arusha Hotel's a good place for cats and friends. The red flowers down in the garden under the good light coming through and knowing now about the cats. It's a hard thing, not so hard you can't get it but it's as difficult an animal to get as you can, remember they're cats.

The buffalo hunt was good, as good as it gets for the male cats and the last hunt was good, it's something about the female's shoulders when she gets low and how they stop and how, when decided, there's no quiet, just a headlong go till death. I want it to be that way, it feels that way now, with what I've committed to it. I've already made up my mind and not jail, not dying, not work, or decree or anything is going to stop this; I enjoy it too much and it's begun to feel like it's capturing something inside and letting it out, what it is, I can't explain, but I know the names of my next two: *The gerbil chronicles* and *Cairn's blacks*.

I haven't bothered with caps just yet as it doesn't feel right until the books have been begun, but if history... everything I've said I'd do has gotten done in the last three books, so I'll trust that.

While others are worried about paying hookers for dialogue I'm just getting it down drip by dogged drip until I've got a cupful. Yeah, I'm off to Cairns in October for the blacks. I've had my shot at the blues in Macao and it's been a dream since I first got the boat. Just checking through the view counts on Youtube it's hard imagining if anyone will give a shit about another field and stream nonsense about fish, but I think I can beat that easily. It's only when you just get out there and do it half-assed that interesting things happen, and since it's not planned and it's writing with all the capitals, it'll do just fine, of that I'm sure.

It's just that I have too many months, it only takes about a month to pound these things out and I like it that way, we're drawing here, carving the loam out of the walls and adding blown ash and rubbing and scuffing and heel of hand to cavewall griming it in. It's the only thing that'll do now, after all the MFAs keep popping themselves out and standing to and being obedient with it I think you know it's time to keep it like this: not real, just drawn. Un-bevel, un-time the damn thing and make it feel it has a pulse and the granite will fall, the love for the granite will just fade, trust it.

I'm going to beat the funniest of books with *The gerbil chronicles*, it will be ostensibly about hate but what'll really be about is me, just self-effacing enough that little Colden will make it out of his self-delusion that he's the best and will sneak through.

Maybe you beat *Midsummer's* or *Quijote*, you never know, with funny there seems to be no limit, in calc it's a strange thing when the function is not defined, that's what probably makes it so hard and why drama and tragedy is so different, you seem contained and inscribed within a known condition–humor leads at its limit directly to insanity and tragedy to sorrow; one boundless, the other sleep.

When we finally lost the male cats after the buffalo hunt we tried and tried and nothing. Then we heard the strange sound, at first with the hunt and with the concentration on the cats I didn't hear it and then I listened.

"What is it?" Keto said.

"I don't know," I said. I wanted to know but it was just so damn strange a sound. I thought hissing at first but when you're out in the bush it didn't make any damn sense. We were down a mobile camp road where the cats had been and we'd driven all the way up to the camp and it was torn down and the metal from the shade canvas was on the ground and all the vanity bulbs on the road in were pulled out and it was a derelict camp, so the sound wasn't coming from there.

Then I remembered the hot air balloons and I said it. It seemed to make sense, "They're filling them," I said. I kept waiting for the big bubble to right itself up the hill, over the horizon. And it didn't happen and it didn't happen. And then I thought something stupid about a gas line, it was a hiss after all, but decibeled and pitched and filling so completely the whole damn bush that it felt all around us and not from one just source. Goddamn.

Keto was just looking funny and keeping quiet about it and then we took to driving down the main road to get after the sound. It was slow uphill jaunt and the sound just got worse, stronger and more hissful and I'd told him about a plastic pipe just sticking out of the ground that I remembered and I was pulling at straws but

I was sure it was a gas main because of the droning hiss and when we crested the hill we saw them

All the gnus of the world, that's what Keto called them once and switched back to "wild-a-beast". A herd to make you cry, the whole hill after hill dotted with them. It seemed there was no way the sound could be theirs. Animals couldn't make this sound, it was industrial and hydraulic at best and as loud as anything a cicada could do in the South times a zillion. Deafening doesn't get it, it was a sound as thick as the bush and the more we drove into the herd, the more it differentiated, a bleating to make you cry. They do this shit between huffing and bark-snoring that's inward I thought, but after watching their diaphragm it's an outward push of wind and each one with a sound as deep or strident as their personalities.

Then we were in it and it's as strange a thing as I can describe, I didn't know animals could make a sound to deafen the ages and quiet the bush and shut off the mind. Keto loved crossing the Landrover an unswollen creek with some luckily well placed rocks. We'd driven down to the water after passing a pride of 11 cats that climbed up the rocks and waited for another car to come down since we were still without the 4WD and when they did we fjorded and then crested in 1 low and the car did that delicious low rumble where each tire is doing what it should and grabbing just perfect and drove into them. They were everywhere, I read they call them blue wildebeest and white striped and all these other idiosyncratic names but what they were was thick. Standing and quelled of their normal trodden run when I'd seen them crossing with the zebra the last trip we made to the Serengeti. Nothing shy about these, everywhere, little ones, big ones, all the ones. It took until the bitter end to get them, when I started looking at them between the bouts of boredom of chasing the cats and the hunts. They had harems just like the impalas, except we'd seen one go from 10 to naught in quicktime. They stand in groups where the bleating males corral their females and their kin and chase off the other bachelors. It's not really that, they chase off anything that moves, the car moves and they charge the car until they get the full implication of the size of this steel beast by Toyota and then they stand and just trot with you and hold their ground.

It seems the females break ranks between surreptitious mouthfuls of grass to go with the males they feel best with, so a dude can go from 10 to none in a blink and then just stares forlornly and goes back to being a sorry ass looking bachelor. Some of them just stand there in the middle of a big nothing after the migration has moved through and bleat at nothing with their patch of grass as if it's worth defending and needful of it when there's nothing around but their imminent death when the cats move through and take all of them. Keto called them the resident males, I always thought of them with a deep misplaced sadness, since their lot is decided and there will be no breeding and no lineage from here on out.

These are the rules, but I break them: always a new city and never go back. It gives me Goa and Muscat and others all the way back to Havana and Confites. I'm not saying it's a good morning, glowing haze like with the cats in the grass but it's what I can manage and it's what's given me this thus far, and it's good, damn good. You're scared a little at first, with the solo part of it and the strangeness, you've always been, Istanbul the first time with her and the Yukon later but that first drive into Mex with the jeep and the screaming cicadas when you had to stop and you were doing your first book in the back vinyl seat at the rest stops in the rain on the red Olivetti; you still got it in you after all these years, deaths delivered, promenades of going with the delicious watermelon feel of the dripping down your chest that's as alive as the rain bouncing off the black vinyl top and you still have how your hips felt jammed between the bucket seats and laying on your back in the no-light of the streetlamp as you pounded away at the rest-stop light coming in the back faded window vinyl, Pop said it: "No other first times, son." And now this, alive with it, the death of it, that hallowed secret you didn't want to give up in your last book and to hell with it, give it to them, let them have it finally, you can afford it now. Why keep it? Why keep old death for yourself only, they suck it up like morning glory in the Canyon and you had it to yourself with the elk in December in the Covid abscess of the lodge with just the crazies and the regulars. And what else is there with the snow crunching on the walks and getting lost in the darkness on the walk back from the too-stuffy restaurant, your only time to get back to the windows open and the haunting light and wheeze of the wind over the eaves. "No other first time, son." Say it again, Pa.

The bullshit of the Schengen means I can step on European soil between the 28th and the 30th, the 30th just to be safe and there's no war to go back to. Kyiv is still burning, but it's a different burning now, the diplomacy has settled things; Finland and Sweden want in and how can you blame them? The only thing is, he's said, "No military infrastructure." These impasses will be dealt with through the normal channels. I can't get my mind off the cats and the fish of Cairns since I committed to this.

It's a funny thing, and I am saving it for *The gerbil chronicles*, all the real funny shit and not the shiftless ironies I'm always pointing out and can't find a goddamn original way to segue into it, so I'm damned with: 'it's a funny thing', but I don't give a shit. There's some things you just have to live with, concessions with your loved ones, your kids who you grow to love, it's never the ocean or the industrial hiss of the migration over the hill, it's just there and you take it, you walk with it, it's your air and there's nothing you can do about it.

Here's another friend: Ari. He had beautiful black hair I was jealous over and had gotten to turning his lip from the video of *White Wedding* and tore the sleeves of black shirts, and then we both ran around like that, tagging churches and corners in the dead of night to feel bad, but we weren't. The only bad I could find was being mean to my mother for loving me and the damn hard part of doing it in spite of losing my dad to his heart when he went on his long dive from the bar and smoked and drank himself to death. But how can you blame him? We're all doing it in our own way anyhow, so Ari's thing was lying and I hated it. It wasn't the psychopathic version, just old-fashioned embellishment to make yourself bigger. The one that really got me was the dolphins.

The girls were somewhere in Florida, we were out on my uncle's boat, Homosassa, I think and they were a daughter and her friend, a little older, that age that gets you starting in on them where a year is a like a decade and if you're a boy you don't know what to do and they do and they're just waiting.

I was quiet and they were asking.

"My father has them in our house."

"Really?" Francis says.

He always made it worse and I got livid.

"Yeah, he built a pool in our backyard."

"How many?"

"Three now."

I couldn't take it and even writing it now, almost 40 years later I couldn't see the joy in the bullshit, my uncle would have loved it, but I never did. You can't love a lie, ever.

It happened one afternoon at Abuito's. I loved the cold nap of the rug in the hot afternoon and somehow we had gotten fried chicken which was hard to get and usually meant finagling an aunt, 'cause Grandma was tight and I remember three pieces and when they said share, I jumped him, not for fried chicken, goddamnit.

It only got worse when we were back in PR, this time I got on top of him and choked him. He'd gotten me good one time when I put him in a full nelson from behind and he flipped me over on my back and knocked it all out of me. I was on the floor, looking up at my father, wanting him to do something and he was just drinking a beer, noncommittal, as noncommittal as you can be and I was raging inside with the shit of 'defend your son' and him just standing there. He never even said anything. I might have said something, who knows, but it felt like betrayal but I learned quick you had to deal with your own shit. I did eventually and it was in the parking garage, me telling him, "What are you going to do now?"

He just called my Ma the other day asking where I was. These are old deaths, and old friends. The oldest die the hardest. The hardest part was seeing his brother that day when I was walking the dog with my mother and he pretended not knowing me, it's the strangest shit when you figure out other people's bullshit. It gets so strange you just begin to roll with it and you leave all your sanctimonious bullshit behind where you wanted everyone to tell the truth all the time.

It's gotten so that you can figure it out with just the smallest of clues, like with his brother, how the car pulled forward and his father didn't get out, meaning he saw you and said he wasn't getting down to say hi to Momma. You know things now, things people are too dumb to tell you, straight up, be it, it's not worth it. So he pretended not to know me and even asked, it's a bad thing to see it done so poorly and it explains the dolphins and how they lost their mother to the bottle because the father was an ass and made lying an endemic family shit like the Manischewitz in the square bottle at the table and the new wife you had to call "Mother". I've gotten good and lax with it now, you forgive them their bullshit easier, you have your father's long slow honest drive and your mother's strangest of honesties, the one of loving you in spite of the rage at losing him. He had a good side in spite of the dolphin shit, it was one thing said in the bathroom of Buxeda where my father was laid up with all the formaldehyde or whatever they stuff them with. He wanted me to grieve proper and I'd just managed a scream, some deep shit out of the howling waste with a word attached to it: "No!"

Ari wanted it again so he took me into the bathroom and told me, "You gotta cry, man."

Even in PR we talked this mean American English and always sounded like we were far away.

"Yeah, dude," I told him.

I had to fake it and somehow managed to cry and we hugged and I felt strangely better and I loved him then and the dolphins and the fried chicken and all the lying to the girls didn't mean shit. There was something true in Ari that day, a deeper caring than I've ever heard, we were only 10. For 10, it's a big man that can tell another boy to cry to get it out; true fucking concern. You know how they say that, 'How do you know if your first one is the one?' They're talking about love and finding it and that first time may be the one, "No other first time, son." Yeah, Pa.

It was the howling waste Randy had fallen into when he took Cass from the back. It's a hard thing to live with and a harder thing to know. And the hard part is living with it. How, whatever twisted shit you've got inside of you, you're going to be drawn to precisely that which you covet. God bless you, if you find it, you may have to start with my two rules just to get away, welcome to Kyiv, our Kyivs.

~~~~~~~~

I still have the Van Gogh thing to do in the bush, but the bush hasn't cooperated, well, the bush has but the chromebook is a no-go. I can't get a mobile hotspot out of Keto's phone sideways, no matter how much cajoling. It may be something about Tanzanian cell service or something on his plan that won't allow it, in any case I'm stuck with none and it's damn annoying.

Sometimes I'm almost alone with Keto out there in the car with me, it feels that way because of the writing and going back in your head to these times that you've confabulated to mean something only to you but with the hindrance, and the necessary one of the foil and the other. There really is never another when you're writing, it's the most selfish of acts and the hardest to pull off if you've got the balls to make it real. The real part is hard as shit and comes almost as rarely as the glow on the prisoners in the one in Paris at the Louis Vuitton, that's the dark room with just that painting. Who's to know they'd discover this about his paint and how he laid it on and what it does if you shine it just so. But I will paint for you and am trying, but to get just a little of this is a rarity that goes beyond language, at least you have an idea from the marl that gets knocked off when you stand up to the cave and have a go at it. I was going to say effluvium but I'd made up a word *efflum*, I needed the hard sound on the end and the strangeness of it and had to settle with changing the whole meaning of the sentence, these are private wars and no damn narrative when it comes down to it. I'm only lucky, once in a hundred pages if I get straight storytelling without all the adornment. It's why I like the girl and the boy book so much, even though it's fake as shit as I know nothing about anything I'm writing it has the tang of the honest story where you're in it; the only part that drove me crazy with satisfaction was the love scene on Ereta and how honest I'd made it. If I can pat myself on the back ever for anything it's that it seemed truer about love what I'd written than anything before or since. The power is what we've been forgetting and the dynamic of it in love; not Miller, not anyone, not Reage, nobody got it. It's a book ultimately about power and a long, slow dive itself about a country coming to terms with its new self.

The British had to do it when they realized the sun does begin to set on their empire, and so will we. Only that ours is a cultural empire and one that wanes and waxes all that more stealthily and propitiously, if you let it. We're just in the heads of people at this point and this seems to be fading fast. You want love, always have and always will, the getting it is the hard part and unless you're willing to kill to get it you have to settle.

Speedy. He lived in the same building as Randy and me and Ari liked him and everyone used to come over for the A/C in his corner apartment. Then we stuck around when he got the dinghy from his mother and we had a way to get out to the reefs without having to paddle out. He used to wrestle and would rub your head hard with his knuckles after grabbing you and we were all afraid of him because of how strong he was from the wrestling.

Looking back he had to be a 180 pounder back then, and I was a big 145, as big as you could be at 5'9" and still get leverage, the difference was Speedy's size and how he'd get you from grabbing you and how good he held on. The good thing is we didn't have to worry about it 'cause he loved us. We were all a tight crew and because he was crazy as shit from a bad divorce and we all knew crazy pretty good from our own shit. From Ari's mother's drunks where she had to be peeled off her piano in the middle of Saturday Night Live when I went over, which I couldn't stand and all the other gringo shit of watching Mookie bat and what Cable did to you when you had it. I was too busy hanging off the backs of cars with my friends from the wrong tracks that when I look them up today–you'd be surprised what you can find with the right keystrokes, their kids are being charged with murder 2. I can't name names and you can see the unfairness of it, these kids taught me to grow up, yeah they were dangerous, and yeah, I loved the shit out of them, and yeah, I had two Jekyll and Hyde worlds to growing up, it always happens in the privates when you're missing a dad and Ma comes in at 10 with the

eczema all over her face from the stress of having to
raise me by herself.

It happened to Jim Wood and his mother was
with the airlines, and his dad died too, and he was the
only other one and it kept us tight, tight with the girls
and starting to chase them before anyone else and getting
them over and having us in the closet to watch. You do
cruddy stuff when you're a kid growing up fast.
Sometimes I look them up and they're photogs in NYC
or they've got their own lives with children and you feel
bad about the shit you put them all through and you need
your boat and Cuba more than ever.

It's a strange thing about drawing all these
connections out of the story about cats and Kyiv and a
dead dad and missing your kids, but it's all you've got.
A couple of wry jokes running around in your head
about the names of kids you grew up with and all the
death that gets thicker the older you get and the more
you try to stay whole and entire, like a fucking country
trying to love itself again, no other first time, son.

And sure, you're unsure of it, if it's even the right
time to propose it. Is it really as dead as you think? The
straight narrative, you're in the forest with the pine
needles and the forest floor and the map and the road
down below, can you still believe all that shit, I never
had, especially all the war-torn narrative, I've no idea
how all these doddering senators can, I just can't get it,
it's almost a strange prehistoric invective against the true

sages and the true original war yarns. Can you give up so easily on Achilles and Homer, goddamn? You've got them, you really truly do, they're still alive in us and deserve reading. It's strange as shit that they aren't *rendido homenaje* more than they should.

It's all you've got, the good life, the good fight when you do fight it and then some. A good wife, just maybe, I haven't found one and if anything's an indication of anything, that may be gone too. The whole thing seems torn, the family thing, the wife thing, even the war thing. They had me going good in *To Kyiv,* I believed it and then you had to go full chess on them and think your way out of that paper bag you were breathing into, goddamn, they almost had you. You would have gone and been happy to die giving it, had the Schengen shit not gotten in the way, it'd been Bulgaria, by way of Sophia or some other non-signed country with intent that let you in. Even the Secretary of State had used the city for their half-assed attempt of shoring up the diplomatic borders, but we're not here for that, we're here for friends and cats and the almighty bush, so let's.

It's been a long dream and one hard coming, just one goddamn story, as real as it gets, as true as true can be and as granitic as the dreams you have for it–give it, thou holy seance, muse of bush. Maybe this is why you'd gotten yourself so deep in it, the commitment does strange things to you, it did in Mex with the waves that can kill you and did and almost did and what really happens on shore, that you promised yourself, if you ever wrote a book about it, it'd start with the kids it truly attracts and how they're killing themselves on shore with the drugs and the fast girls and how you have to speed for the wall at a 100 to even have a shot, but that's another book you've always wanted and hasn't shown itself and waits.

~~~~~~~~

I loved her shoes first, silver patent leather lace-ups that reminded me of the Doc Martins, just the laces and she had the strangest way of lacing one handed, a loop with a half-hitch and one ear and then the other of the rabbit, you'd have to see it done to believe it, there are reasons for lacing with one hand and I can write stories for the reasons, a broken arm that never healed or a termagant that forced her with one hand or just the damn tradition that is different, whatever it is: love. You felt it, son, again, in the dark and then in the dark and then again in the sleep, and then again waking, and then in the early light from the curtains that you cracked to let in the rainy early light of Arusha.

It is storming today, but it's a coffee storming, just wet good weather for the beans to make it in the hills and it must have been this way in Yabucoa when your great grandpaps started. I've read by way of the great Dominican historian that there was also ginseng, but the

Island had to survive on something other than cane and coffee and what little tobacco, and so he did and so you do, now, with what little love has come your way. Your learning kid, the cats have to learn after every hunt, and they did.

The absolute first hunt was perfection of form and only twenty minutes of glassing can give you what a cat can do in the tall grass. When she's committed and she was, she started with the stares from the tree, I had to fight with Keto about not giving up. We were about 250 yards downhill from the only game which were 5 zebra and they wouldn't come down from the top part of the hill, so every time she slept and popped up it must have never looked good enough to start so she didn't.

And then she did and I told Keto, "There she goes." And she came walking toward me after arranging to pick her up at 8:30, and her scarf was a deeper vermillion than blood in the sun and it was a puffy soft scarf and she got in next to me, Doudas had been generous and we had the wide strange back seat of the Toyota minivan, accent light up every pillar and you know by how a girl hugs you what night it's going to be. I was back in the part of his book when he had to use the leather holster and its hardness and how she would sidle up to him to give you an idea of how he felt about her, but then he might have gone a little nuts with the shit of shaving her head. She looked fully Maasai but wasn't, popping dreads that came up straight, 3 and half and fun to play with and it's a funny thing how you met in front of the ice cream store. You'd told Doudas and he has the sugar problem but took you anyway, with the shit of the high bar being set with Haagen Dazs and then brought tumbling down from your half a year in Baires at Freddo's you can only be disappointed.

It was a dark place when we walked in and as big as a dancehall and just as forlorn once it empties the next day if you walk in to clean it down. 5 or 6 and you walked up to what was fresh in the tills, and it looked like all the bad ice cream that's too sweet in Plaza Loiza when you're really looking for the homegrown guanabana, soursop for you lesser souls and of course, with no Swahili, Doudas ordered and you were pissed again from mixing the three flavors in the tumbler and then the squirt of chocolate and you took it outside with the two chairs to watch Arusha go by and then you saw her, and sweets, my darling, you look and the shit is exchanged and you always know and you called her and it was on for 8:30 and then you're in the dark, the real true dark. There's a thing that happens, when you get to be a kid again, like the first time and she told you after the fourth dark, "nakupenda" and she meant it and you said it back and you can, even now love someone like this, this far away from everything and that it be true, no other first time, son.

The cat does a funny thing with her shoulders when she's committed to the idea. I was just remembering Doudas going crazy after picking us up in the morning wanting the low-down. I'd given up on my father's patrician ways of keeping shut about the conquests.

"You know what she told me?" Doudas was earnestly asking.

"Tell me."

"It's the first thing she said when you got in the car. 'That you know how to fuck', that is good, my friend. 'And that you're sweet'," and we started laughing

No other first time, boy. Goddamn.

The cat had two cubs under a tree with some LandCruisers that had given up on them and left and they only popped their heads up when they weren't sleeping. When you see a cat hunt like this, with this determination it's for her kids, and it's the same through all this dark we went through, do you think you'll keep and she'll let you keep it when they come. Then the real hunting begins and the dross gets ladled aside, live with it.

It was a good holdout all these years. You went back to your early days in Zipol when you were so crazed with it, the loving and the drugging and the waves that watching Noah roll in the dirt with the old dude in the boots was as pure as it got. Or Pancho peeing on the feet of the fresa of his opening night of his disco in Oaxaca. It's told now in the dark, through the line of you, you cat, you're on their walls now, "he knows how to fuck", talc and gypsum and loam and marl and crudded ash of firestick. And this is what you leave now, all in the heads of these girls and your son, your sea and she's still on me as I write this, all night on her chest and starting with the close forehead to lips sleeping, me underneath, I prefer it that way and the dark was as good as wood when you drilled your boat for the underwater lights and it took you back to 1961. What year are you at now, boy?

Her shoulders came up and that cat walked in the grass from one tree to another. When you're glassing all you see are the black felt tips of her round ears and only then for brief flashes, if not her back and the shoulders. At a 100 yards it's still clear, at 150 through these yellow binoculars you only get a little of the cat, it's almost just a splash of the caramel coat against the light green of the grass or the blowing soft red tops of the grass that is no red at all and just helpful when looking for their game trails to see what was tamped down.

And she came in the dark, over you, on the fourth and fifth dark, and there's a way she can walk where it hits her just right, and she purrs, I can't say what purr it's like, it's too profane for even a book and you just let it, it's all coming down and you have to let it. Dark on dark now and when you get her over and just right, a waist of dark and you hold on, like breath to her she's still walking in the grass and you can barely see her now, you're over 200, you need to know where she is and any wave of grass and that's all you have to know where she is. She's leaving now, and all you can do is look for the zebra and watch what they do, ironic, it's a white horse with black stripes, but so it goes, the dark is the irony and you're so deep in it, just the thought of her is a hunt.

Winnie Joel. God, this Christmas. Death and dying now. It's the only approach, you go down to the shore and the dock your father made of you with the contact sheet and the AE1, slow dives, and slow this one, the dark, pushing on the dark, wanting so deep in the dark you're up against nubbin and you know how to push it and the cat purrs, the grass does and the white horse bucks and she's on her back, white from the glassing and dust is coming off her and she bucks her off and then the stand-to, 50 off watching defiant, *haw-hawing* about it and bitchingly defiant, you would have run and not stopped. Just that now you're going down with it, any slightest of affronts and we're taking it down, be damn the lightning and knowing how and what was going to take you.

You felt foolish at the doctors for the HIV, waiting for the lilac creep of the ink up to the control line and hers drew first, Winnie Joel, and now you, you know what's taking you out. Not the gun, not the water, not you, the air's taking you out, and this cat in the grass. She's slowly coming back, walking back to a further tree, lavender cat, purple with it, the surety you'll get them the next time and so it creeps this draw of blotted blood up the paper to tell you what you'll die from, son.

And you did in the dark with her, your cat, this your Arusha, dear sir. The ledger you wanted, the selfsame signature you wanted so badly to see and did, with her. How can you explain it, Confites?, all the traveling, the leaving, the leavening of you and your back to this, love, son. Love, nakupenda, not fisi, not mzuri but this, dark globes like shaken pewter light, but darker, a lot darker, it's water, remember and warm, you drowned in it as a kid and then some, and later on the 25th after the first book and you're drowning again now in the dark, but there's breath here and breathing. The cat has laid down and in less than thirty minutes she will hunt again.

It starts when she sees them sleeping, she will wait and they will walk right over her and almost step on her and again she will jump on one and again they will buck and gallop off and this time leave dead serious, turning up the hill and going off with a halter of dust kicking up to her neck. White horse with black stripes gone on a jaunt to another valley and this time the cat walks to the hill and crests it and goes over and there's no game road to see her off. At our best from the car we had four cats, the three you know and one cheetah that would head-pop a good half a mile off and then I saw her on a keeled over tree standing proud and looking into what she would be walking toward.

Which is ours? Our tree keeled over that we're standing on, looking out before going into it, the fingers are tired today, the dark has done that to me. Even the booking is difficult on the mobile app, the whole thing is conspiring to get you to move and go into, another trip to the bush but the nights are so warm in Arusha and the days so wet, a tropical forest, good for coffee and pining of home with the fast road to el Yunque. And so you go toward it, we always do, unceasingly, profligate with it, that the joy encountered will somehow supersede all the others.

A little boy runs the beach, his boxer running behind him, Attila gallivanting, kicking up the sand and now he's really running and you can't see the intelligence anymore, not even in the people or the cats, things just are and he jumps and you're turning and punching, his chest as hard and birdlike as an ostrich, and the fury won't let up and the guy on the trike this morning who when you asked about the FSB to get money out pulled matches and a joint and you saw the loped off finger and it took a good 5 minutes 'cause your phone doesn't even work and the Whatsap's storage is full and she doesn't know how to use Messenger even though she has it and it's a discombobulated fuck of a time until you get this Swahili down and then you think fuck it, tell him to come here at 8:30 and you'll go with him to go get her. It's what the bush has done to you, frayed the edges and taken it completely off. You're starting to warn people, it's real, if you think I don't mean it, it's best not to find out. They think you're a tourist and you keep telling them you're not, you've been this way since Zipol and the crazed and beautiful part of it is, what keeps this glaze from shattering is only will and enough love to not go ham on the whole thing, and now that you've found it, a little love with the dark and your back is showing it, the way your shoulders come up as you go toward that which is remorseless, all of us, now in double-time, and we pray and hope and "if you know me," your telling Doudas this, "it's come undone," it did a long time ago and it shows and yet it remains, is still a story and you've changed it, the promise and premise you started with has come true, the price your mind, but you never had it anyhow and the light carafes through the pulled shade.

When you wake with the bullshit 7:15 *takiti-takiti*, reach and tap and hug her one more time and another and smell her and feel Mehru and Kili and goddamn, a real one, again my boy, again, and you crack that shade and she knows to hit the vanity light on the look at yourself closely mirror, good blue avatar light and we shower, this time both of us and she gets out to *cepillar* in front of the mirror when you make it up for her and then the funky soap that you press out of the dispenser and her back, smooth as stones on a river and when you towel off and go back the light is good and then you can open and Arusha, you beauty and just the best and you know it, the coffee tells you so and the rain and the blue light and the quiet city and her and you and you're repeating because you don't have to, known now, de Kooning known and the work has become second hand, imagine waiting in a cage to get out 20 year, 30 year and now here, what must it feel like? This mountain, of you, Mehru on her again and you fall to the bed one last time, minutes counting, downstairs by 8:05 and Messenger from Doudas, go motoboy, so you trike it and goddamn, it's lovely to go out into it this way, it's been 4 safaris and you're spoiled rotten with the comfort of it and now her, light is changing now, what was a wet and tree-dripping morning has let the light in and the banana leaves take umbrage with it and you must think *platanos* and cooking and boiling and unstringing the most beautiful golden food and ketchup of course but no, light through a banana leaf is a truth, older and more self-evident than man, gone now, that's how fleeting and you wonder as you wrote about it, how long will this one last, "mtoto?" you want to ask her, and will and then of course, "napenda." Is there anything else to it? Why not, as Keto would say.

The cats of Manyara must have jumped the zebra and when you got there they were already tearing into her and the red flower near the banana leaf has come up again and the tubas have started in Arusha, just out of town and then it comes in all its glory and it starts suddenly like the craziness of a Jodorowsky film. All fun and romp and Mexican festivity, it must abrade a lesser soul, this refusal to commit to the narrative but fuckit, they must understand what's changed, who's to compete with the celluloid, and even if you did, why? Even they can't and what's more, it's been done as well as it can be and plus, this is me, as she stands, and she refuses and what can you do? So I don't, I just get washed with it, just a hum of tune walking down the parapet of Misiones and *takiti-takiti* and you look at the blue numbers and tap and now you must go, your hands can't leave this, dark and she says it in the shower, "white and black", white horse and black stripes and the zebra's come undone and stands there, four legs in the shower staring down, cloven dreams of blue light.

The dark has come, again, dark puddles and dark feet and dark rain in the dark night. Plodding, tap-tapping with your little feet and you would jump off the stern and tied, towed by the boat your father thought sincere, and you will again with your own son or daughter, and so will they and they will love. You have no past, you told her. Only through the Swahili translate on Google can you make a go of it, Peep through the buds when it's not the rain that you used last night for her headache after the last blue gel cap and then she woke in the dark and giggled and shook, shook hard and the curtains were open, cracked for the city to come in and Arusha shone and so did her stones, on her back, the blue kudu light you were after, you thought you came for the game and now you're here with this and a beginning, only the Ninth, when the chorus begins can give you an idea, so at breakfast this morning you finally got through with the .904 after your name which was a random Facebook choice which just happened to be an old area code when you were after what Tolstoy had to leave to get it: all the gambling to get your soul unstuck and then he committed, and so shall you, now, right here, Peep and Horsehead, buds in your ears telling you so, you used roots in the last book to give Janis the free romp she needed and now you use the rain and the dark to go into the morning and she messaged what she wanted and you committed to it, love, son, no other first time and you're here with it, and *Nakupenda Sana Norman naitaji kuwa na wewe kimausiano napia naitaji mtoto na wewe ukotiali...* and I won't, I'll let it stand as it shone, as bright a light in the dark as ever told, the same Crane saw at the bridge and now an oath as solemn as ever swore and you're a fool to leave it when found again and the luck of it, the Macao luck in October, the luck of the last book he tried to write on the trip to Nairobi when he didn't shoot anything anymore and you're unstuck with it, her back and the stones and the arms have drawn a line in the night only an antecessor in Chauvet could have known, no modern but atruck the ages now, free of it, blessed and beginning and no need to re-dazzle with the carafe you poured a whole book into and look it up and Google translate and you will have the coda to this: me.

The mornings were bright in Inagua. We'd left the salt and the sun shone gunmetal black on the water as we went out. In half an hour you would have him. The Senator screaming with the 100 kilo thread mono from *Marine Dream* you spooled on the dock when your mother brought you with the sack of oranges, *saco de chinas* and you spooled on the back deck of the Chris Craft with the Texan that may have been an islander.

All things contained herein now, torn a long time ago from that boat and how could you have known you'd hook yourself now, kiddo? Come undone have you, fuck'em, if they get it, they get it. If not, walk the galleries, it wasn't Modilgiani, it was his roomie who taught us everything, every day for months in Bellas Artes with Covid and the dumb blue dots on the *marmol* outside in the searing blind white marble heat to get it and there she was, standing, he'd gotten all of it, the only price: hunger, and a wicked mind that must come undone, and you're a paying the price again and oh, so sweet, bring on the dark rain, I'll be that boy in the puddle, I'm looking up at the night, only Vieques and Culebra have it and it's a shock of stars like sprent glass a foundry wheel spinning 'em up to the heavens, little boy, you, up there with it without knowing death come knocking at a Sunday reprieve and you howled and have been howling and now, this night, once more cometh, she's dark and holy and smells of Arushan fields, you'd have to know the way, kiddo, a haltertop when she fell on you with those wicked skates and the roller rink splashed on your face and she kissed you with all the abandon of a plop of a stone on the water, last spinning drop before she sashays and dervishes, you oblong stone to the ones underneath–always a beauty to watch it happen from the dock, watch anything fail and fall, the procession is no clean dive, there's some jingle to it, always something cute and gracious and so it goes, here, now, with it and trusting you'll come undone but like you said when you came here: "I'm no fucking tourist" and you'll die giving it and if they have to test you, you can't wait to flay the sun, bring this joy on, compadre. If I be not complete, not undangerous, then you don't know what dangerous is, what the danger of a man tested is... what the taste of something you've waited all your life to have, what the tongue must feel, what the last breaths, what the joy, of being delivered and to lay, staring at it and to feel home again, and with father and all lost ones. You cannot win, not you, country, nor heathen, nor rage, nor woman. Anytime, anywhere, it's a good day, I kiss you with this, a complete abandon–the only way to live and the legend to this domain. Finally a secret promised delivered, it is love, as malformed and strange and a rock to leaven the ages.

~~~~~~~

Fuck the nakupenda, when you think your girl might be fucking you around because you're the old guy and then you put your thinking cap on and fuck the morning fuck and pull out the cell and Swahili translate, "do you like girls?", I don't know what the fuck the word is but you got the, "yes" and now we have a safari with two of them. Good god, I can't describe the ass on this girl if I tried but in the good light this morning–and I don't know if I can manage the Van Gogh thing with two in tow, if she's anywhere near as pretty as her friend, fuck me, I'm going to die at my father's age under two dark beauties, I don't give a shit. This is what it's come down to. To know you have to know and I know, I'm as ready as I've ever been, no seeing my kids and as far away as you can get without circling the thing and damn, you're doing it kid and they think it's about the money, Doudas thinks it's about the money, the girls and the waiters and old Aziz who reared his little head just now after the debacle with the laptops and you have to understand, they do–I just don't give a shit.

See, the thing is, to know you have to know, it's getting back at the secret I was saying, die under a woman, you'll know, how many of these fucking creeps fucking around on their keyboards will never get a shot at something like is and the old money is still yielding returns and you're making it, kid. Without language, just your cock and a keyboard and some massive balls to end it this way, you had to bring it down, did you... Look, it's not me controlling this, so I stopped trying, if you're not changing by the second, they have you, pegged for this or that, or your too noble and bordering on pushover and stupid or you're not nice enough but you can make it, kid, the girls will take you to the cats and that will be your canvas, two beauties, just think of it, the dark stones on their backs and the hyenas, fisis going *who-hooting* and you just might get it.

What you've been searching for all these years, your line, kid, in Africa, and who would have known, the blue kudu and the rift wall, what's pushing up against what now? It used to be that all the books were about things and you had to try hard as hell to get it and if you couldn't you faked with a pretty turn of phrase, the little bitching, felicitous one and now we're getting it to where you can kind of just let it be and hope and pray this shit you're doing is making some kind of sense and not this monumental waste but see... you can never know, and any theatrics I give you and you just have to let it play out as it stands. All these well-made books and the puffs going about it, shit, don't you feel the empire dying and the staleness of it and here I am trying to crack this precious nut and make it new again, Ezra new, the real new where we letting it all in, a little Whit of vista to this new thing and I'll hope, I really will, maybe the cats or this dark beauty that will soon be two and tell me, who else, Who!?

"Who else?
Who out there is doing it?"

~~~~~~~~

Here he is now at the rift wall with her. Winnie, merry with her and it's a dark world with a dark girl in a dark land. Winnie brought her friend, Neema and they're a good duo, always laughing and two real sweet cons, telling me shit about Oxford and a trip to London for females studies or some shit and Winnie telling me about 'my husband' and all I can think about are the dark rocks on her back and the shit she does to me in the heat of the tent when we break up the safari at 1 for the lunch to die for and then swelter it up with the hottest of naps and if we're not sucking toes or a foot entire we're laughing it up loving the shit we're doing together.

I had it all wrong in the book about the killer when Jani tears up her lover on the rocks above Alicante. See, she thinks it's about possession when it's not, it's all about this give and take shit and it was pointless imagining love could be brought down to earth this way and that the hard shit was where it's at. It's not, take away yourself and just leave your skin and your fingers and your toes and you're halfway there. She'll go crazy if I put her black tit in my mouth and I do it for a full hour. There's things we've done that make me feel like a kid wondering where it's all gone, all those good years fucking yourself up with the bad girls you were supposed to marry and grow old with and here you are in Africa with it, the real shit, the real girl, the real dark girl you've come to, that fucking rift wall you were after and the blue kudu, kid.

I found her, father, I really did. It's like a fucking dream, to get it all back after all these years and the two kids lost to the ether. You never thought you would and here now with the fucking flies and her saying, "Fuck you, butterfly" and you've found it kid.

"Fuck you, butterfly."

Again. "Fuck you, butterfly." And Ezra is with us again, except it ain't the "wet black boughs" or whatever, it's take all that fucking extraneous beauty the fuck out.

Yeah, she texts next to me, something about her modeling agency and yeah, we talk about mtoto, and the house and the life together, and there's nothing you can do when you're stuck in the rip being pulled out to Puerto when it's pounding the sand and making it fly and you're damned if you go out and damned if you try going in, so you just let it. A little sideshore paddle and just hope for the best and that you can relax and make it through and you do. Because you've learned how to breathe and all the hard girls and the hard drugging make it so land is just another shit.

We're at the firepit with our legs up that the Maasai from Ngorongoro, Joshua, stokes and then walks us to our tent with the real Maasai spear. I've held it, a sharp ass blade and some heft to it and a real spear on one end, the other like a Turkish knife. And it's all you've got against the lion. The real lion is you. And you keep telling her you are the bush, when she started in on the iPhone 13 shit when crossing the Naabi gate you lost it again. The first time you had to tell Keto to shut his trap or you were going to fuck him up. And you meant it, a bitch can get you so lost that, you caught yourself singing it, '*I just fell in love with a bad bitch...*' and he was good until he wasn't and then you told him as nice as you could to just not talk to them as it's the drama they're after.

"It's best just to ignore them", and you meant it, you told him you knew him a whole hell of a lot better than them and you think he got it, he really did. You still cared about him as if he was your kid, the same age as Pedro and he fell asleep again on the drive in from Arusha. You'd left Manyara at 5 to make the gate at Ngorongoro at 6 and you got there just in time. All the trucks were waiting and the gate slid open and Keto pushed the LandCruiser through, dodging all the old Detroits. They run the oldest trucks here in Tanzania. Inside Serengeti I've seen shit from the Sixties still going good and like all things worth keeping, the gauge on the steel is as thick as the century you need to keep it going.

He'd fallen asleep again on the drive from the lodge to the gate, Neema even caught it, he was in the wrong lane, foggy and sweet mountain air misting up making it like some fucking dream and Keto went off. I wasn't planning on telling her about it, but she caught it and I think she got what I said about the difference between men and boys. They have a way of not differentiating in cities but here where it matters, it'll kill you. See, Keto is crazy about the massage girl, Anita. They'd gotten their HIV tests and Keto was setting up on her again and it's a funny thing how he's hellbent on living with a good woman, give me the bad ones, I want the pain, fuckit.

I got one white rhino in me, had to tell the waiter extra Kahlua 'cause he didn't want to dirty the milk with the walk uphill to go get it. Peep through the earbuds drowning out the traditional African music here poolside in Manyara and it's almost like reminiscing when he wrote his first story, the breakout, up in little Michigan and he remembers the girl and her look, shouldn't it be that way?, all your glory when you need it, just spinning it up when you need it, at hand, fuck... imagine it that way, all those fucking years trying so hard and it was just you, the first story about the ants and the tree behind Abuito's house. Can you have it? If you really want it? There's no way really, except this one.

Winnie came by way of ice cream, I was outside the ice cream joint up where the Arusha road goes north to Kenya and I saw her walk by, a little precocious and a little jaunty, who knows. Just asked her and we were getting HIV tested later that night at the private clinic and it's never been the same 15 nights later and one safari that started with all the drama you'd expect, fuckit, what else is there? Just dark stones on her back and something if I went into it would break all of writing for all time, so I just might. Think of the Afar and Leakey and what *In the Shadow of Man* did for you and the rain in the forest when you first read it, fuck, kid, you've finally found it, went with this half-assed hope of skirting a war and came to this to find it in the dark of her thighs, fuck 'em, and I mean it fuck 'em all, if all this goddamn propriety brought you to this and now you've found a way to not be such a good boy and damn, they're jiggling in the dance, the drums have come up and now Africa is drowning out Peep and fuck! It's coming like it always comes, life... Life, kid, with all its glory, you've found it again, after 2 bad women and kids you won't see and all this fucking Western expectation and the drums have come up and its your heart kid, beating in her and you had the presumption to ask her in the Swahili translate chat, "How many cattle will you father provide for the wedding?" "40" she said, it's a damn good number and you will find a Maasai boy to tend her dowry and it's a good life once again. She's done things to you no other has, shit's so good you can't think straight and don't want to. Who does?

Damn, kid, your girl's going to get up and dance and knock the socks off all the tourists. You don't like talking, fuck, with an ass like that, doing what it does, why? Tell me, tell me really, why? And I think you know, do you remeber when you dropped Jessie off and went back for her and took her up to Las Gladiolas and the elevator was off and you walked the 15 flights and she had a kid in the crib and told you about her husband in the peni, locked up for some shit and it's all that feeling bad about what you came from and how if you could make it right you would, you know what it is, kid, it's the shit, kid, all the shit they've piled on all these years having us believe there was some truth to it, that what was being said would make it right and somehow it never did, all you have is this now, some half-assed belief in yourself you're going to drill the rock again and come up with it, someway somehow, ore, have you, all of it, and light up the world again, and be damned all of you that don't believe, I am going to die doing it, like I said, a fucking promise to break the whole ether.

She was wearing silver patent leather shoes, laced up and cycle shorts and high purple sheened top and she was happy and in the back of Doudas' car where I sat with her I could have been in the taxi going through Paris like Jake but I picked up where he left off in ...*First Light* and it's all beginning to fade, all the shit you have to deal with when really trying to do this, you have to contend, you really do, the white rhino sauced up is telling you so, your bitches are telling you so, you fought good and hard for them, had to fend off Keto and the city Maasai when the fisi crossed the camp and scared the shit out of them. Hyenas, they call the fisi here, there was some crazy bitch from Spain, I think, who went out into the bush with her long lens to photograph a buffalo–can you imagine?, sneaking up on a buffalo and the fucker charged and all I saw was the chick running out of the bush in front of the tent and the snout-up buffalo huffing and giving the same look they give the lion when they get lit up.

And so it happened with my girls, went off to the tent just before dusk and the fisi crossed at that trot they have where it's a loping run and their half-assed, back fallen, rump dragging run that's somewhere between wicked and gargoyle strange and you believe it, that they'll bit your face off in your sleep if you're not careful. The dancers are beginning to smell, the tourists are wide-eyed with it and it's the smell of man that gets the girls going and damn isn't that what's missing, a little musk to get the girls going? So, the girls went and then I saw Winnie hiding behind the termite mound and I'm like damn, they're just fucking around and then the fisi ran through and fuck, yeah, you got up and that was it, you knew just enough about the damned bush dogs that they weren't after your girls, something else drew them through the camp, maybe cats, maybe some shit going on down the hill, and fuck, 40 cattle's pretty good for Winnie, I mean 40, at 400 a head that's some hard work her father had to put in and you will take it, you will take all of it, always, when it's the way things go, you take it and fuck it, what else is there?

Maybe it'll turn you into a man finally, not all the knives and the guns and all the shit across Mex, not even the waterfront at Barca when the Arabs came for you and tried chopping you down with the sides of their hands against your neck just to see if they could and then drop you in the drink, and not Fatso on the fourtrack somewhere in the swamps of Pasco trying out all the shit on the ducks, and you fired all there was to be fired. 22's, buckshot, 9's, 45's–all of it and when you tell people, fuck if they don't believe, you've done it all, your fingers hurt from waking up with it, the goddamn sugar in your blood these 51 years taking you down with it, but your dive, unlike your father's will have a different grace, was it "the talent of Kipling, and the discipline of Flaubert"? The wrong of it was not to let in the new century, it's hard to read when it's that good, it's all you've got to usher it what's going to kill us. Don't we all know we're going down with it, the whole bleating century with all its promise. What have you, I say? What have you?

It's early in Manyara, we're about to go out on our last day and Winnie and I were Swahili translating the coming child and all her uncertainties. Me going on about the 40 cows and her starting in on a bull for her father and her smart as a whip saying you can't just sit on your ass and not make us a living, and me telling her in chat: I tell stories for people that don't have any. It's not really that fair, as it was a little rehearsed, but fuck, trying to let in the whole damn thing is as selfish as it gets, but that's okay I still love the dark stones on her back.

How to tell anyone what you've found down here, just like that little chat you gave the old lady in the laundry on Great Inagua or was it San Sal?, in any case you told your treasure and the dockmaster came for the gold ass watch with the dates in French and Spanish, damn you!, why couldn't you shut up and now this, telling it to the whole world. Can you even describe it, what it's like with her on top of you dancing that shit into your bones and you feel something in her jiggle on you and it's like a tinkerbell and some fucking rabbit hole you've fallen down with her and she's been behind you, under you, you behind her, ain't no shit you haven't done and all those white bitches couldn't give it to you, truth, the ugly shit at first and it's coming down like rain and you're in the puddles just like a kid stomping away, who knew it could be so good and the safari is over and you're back in Arusha and the shit's come down so hard all you can do is sleep eat and fuck a little, a limp little, she's taken it all out of you and now this, no kudu, all the hunts you could have wanted: two cheetah and one with lion on the way in the Gol Kopje. The cheetah was on the last morning, you lucked into it and the cheetah was off on a lope and popping up on the termite mounds and then you saw the wildebeest all scrawny as fuck, a lone crazy one like always and the wilde' saw what was coming and crossed the road and the cat behind at half-run and then she gave up. The one before, was the day earlier and the cheetah took a whole hell of a lot of time setting up and then she sat a herd of wildebeest and just watching those shoulders come up and down flanking them in the taller grass and you had it again finally, watching something as pure as fuck go at it. All these bullshit safaris–you even told Keto, yours would be called *No Bull* safari and give these people a real run for the money and show them the real shit.

If it was up to you, you'd have tournaments just like in big game fishing and a hunt would be worth so much, a kill even more and the secret would be to get people becoming part of the hunt and to see the cats do what they do best, not this cats laying in the grass shit, where nothing happens, a cat is a killer, straight up, real kill you dead and think nothing of it, you saw a dumb bitch come running out of the grass in front of the tent, imagine trying to photo a buffalo and stalk and then sneak up on it, the buff was huffing with its snout out and all you saw was the dumb bitch loping off with her long range finder and the dumb pants and the dumb shirt and they don't know the first thing about the bush. No matter how hard you'd try with them it would all be for naught. Damn city people have gotten so far from themselves they don't know what's what, just slicking it in the bush–a dude with the arm tats and the blue hair and the Malcolm x hard rims and had his beer in the firepit and I wanted to screenshot from the chromebook and piped up and he said, "shift control" and some other shit and I was like, "It's a chromebook," then he talked about the high six figures his sister was making to the dude next to him and how I wished I hadn't taken Peep off the loop I had him on to keep the others away. Even the chick that had run from the buff came over and sidled off when they heard it, I mean, yeah, I had my shirt unbuttoned and Winnie with her high wool socks and the Cookie Monster green sweater and her purple skirt and her done-up gamey hair all spikey and red burnt and Neema with a new wig every day and it's a trifecta of crazy if you ever saw it and you would to, skip a beat and go back to the lodge and have dinner proper at a table, leave the fisi and the firepit and the Maasai that are coyly flirting with Winnie and fuck it, we are going to Mwanza to see her Baba and Mama and settle up and we're after a home now in Arusha in the rain and it's all you can do these 51 to keep the swan dive from hitting the water full bore and blown to bits, smithereens, all that fucking grace, you'd had and lost a thousand times and who's to know and how, that it'd be you to break the century in with paint flinging words on the canvas of now. Fuck yeah, doubt it, it's all catch-up from here and you know it and can feel it, 'cause it's real this time, bitches, you know 'cause you know.

From constrained to the succubus of this fetish of wrapping it tight to now, the whatever, we're undone with it, just flinging it and whatever, like I give a fuck, can you when you're crashing into the wall and she's all over you, black dark stones on her back, smelling like dark turned earth and in her a *'fuck you butterfly'* to make you cry, motherfuckers, have it?

*Kuelewa*, do you get it, kid, Swahili now to this and the paint flies like it should, all of it, through all time and there's not stopping it now, not rabbits, not nothing– we're trying to find a house in Arusha to play it the way it should, the normal way of going about the boy girl shit and setting up shop, the same way the cats set up and go about it except I want that relaxation they get, that laying in the sun after the hunt and the kill inside of them. Where's that?, yeah, you've tried, too many times to say fuckall and give it another go, but yeah... one more, kid, she loves you, the laptop on your chest told you so, when she said look at the Prados and you're like what?, how can you get angry with all the shit you've been through and seen, the clicked nines to your head, the selfsame bullshit when you were 21 and had two Porsches and 2 MGs parked one street down and you had to choose what and what color to drive... how can you, really? Angry at what, fuck all of you and your judgement, I mean it, hate this? Love in all its form and refracted back from the dhows sailing down from Muscat and the unloading of dried sundries and you're like what? What, motherfuckers? Don't you get it, the blue kudu, the rift wall, 'fuck you butterfly' and the two dark stones on her back and the smell of her before the rains. Now do you see what the rains bring?

It rains past judgment and past the whole shelaqued bullshit we've called books until now, don't fear yourself in them, it's what we're really after, we really want to know if it's you and what you're really like, bare it, it's the new demand, music and the show and tell of the boob tube caught up, now it's up to you, kid. Show it, all of it, move those two dark stones and tell them what if was like with her on top of you jingling that bell tolling for thee, aha, aha, now, kid, they're the steps of the kudu in the early blue light, just outside your door when you're moving the catch with your foot and didn't see it, and didn't see it, damn you father, a long slow fucking dive on the burnt bar with the grasshoppers with crème de menthe you made Mother and the cigars you smoked when I came out in Pavía in the hospital and you had to drink it up and I've this penance, this godforsaken curse of having to do this with no choice, not one fucking choice, not México, not Oaxaca and all the arcilla burnt thumbs in the halflight with Nacho and the fuckit you gave yourself from 24 until you rounded that corner and made it out of the bullshit and had your sea legs and started on a family at 31 and here again and you've told her, "I am the bush" and there's no way out, cars and houses and iPhone13 and you're like–she'll get caught up in it and then it'll be too late, when they realize you were mist, wanting something made it and *te esfumas*, there's no other way.

Made in the USA
Columbia, SC
09 November 2024

18bcc1be-c638-4d46-8750-cb89187eea8cR01